GETTING STRAIGHT ABOUT THE BIBLE

GETTING STRAIGHT ABOUT THE BIBLE

HORACE R. WEAVER

Nashville   ●   ABINGDON PRESS   ●   New York

Getting Straight About the Bible

Copyright © 1975 by Abingdon Press

Library of Congress Cataloging in Publication Data
Weaver, Horace R
    Getting straight about the Bible.

    Includes bibliographical references.
    1. Bible and science. 2. Bible—Study.
    3. Eschatology—Biblical teaching.
    4. Religion and astronautics I. Title.
BS511.2.W4   220'.07   75-2342
        ISBN 0-687-14138-9

Manufactured by the Parthenon Press at
Nashville, Tennessee, United States of America

To
Cheryl Weaver de Zayas and Luis de Zayas

CONTENTS

PREFACE 11

HOW DID IT ALL BEGIN
(A Modern Study of Genesis)

Introduction 13
Let There Be Light 17
And There Was Light 19
God Created the "Heavens and the Earth" 23
God's Design for Matter 24
Creation of Living Beings 29
The Miracle of Reproduction 34
Created in His Image 36
God's Mighty Acts in Creation of Life 38
Person's Responses in Faith and Love 41
Suggestions for Group Discussion 45
Notes 45

DO YOU USE OR ABUSE THE BIBLE
(Letting God Speak Through Its Pages)

Effect of Attitudes 46
What Is the Bible? 49
How Was the Bible Written? 53
How Luke Wrote His Gospel 54
How First and Second Chronicles Were Written 55
How the Pentateuch Was Written 57
Why Inconsistencies Exist 59

The Importance of the Medium 60
How Were the Books of the Bible Chosen? 63
The Canon Is Fixed 67
Some Abuses of Scripture 70
Eisegesis or Exegesis 74
Value of Historical Criticism 76
Eisegesis on the Birth of Satan 78
Science and the Bible 81
Suggestions for Group Discussion 83
Notes 84

WHAT ABOUT THE RAPTURE, THE SECOND COMING, 666 ...
(Finding Meaning in Apocalyptic Literature)

Two Views of Our World 86
How Does One Get Close to God? 89
The Ascension and the Kingdom of Heaven 90
Jesus Christ the Lord Reigns 92
Prophecy and Apocalypse 94
Daniel—Stories And Visions Of Loyalty And Hope ...100
Revelation—Letters from John to His Churches 105
The Two Beasts of Revelation 107
A Modern Message via Apocalypse 111
John's Creative Use of His Old Testament 113
The Rapture 117
Things That Are to Be (Eschatology) 119
Suggestions For Group Discussion 122
Notes 123

EXTRATERRESTRIAL LIFE AND INTELLIGENCE
(Christian Faith Can Cope with It)

The Whole Universe Is Full of God's
  Creative Acts 125
Intelligent Life Throughout the Universe? 128
The Nature of Spiritual Beings Created
  in the Image of God 130
How Would We Communicate with Space Beings? ...133
NASA's Hopes to Communicate 134

Suppose God Has Created Intelligent Beings
  Throughout the Universe 137
The First Interplanetary Conference on Faith 139
God's Concern for Freedom 149
The Uniqueness of Faith 150
God Seeks Covenant Relationships 151
Suppose an Extraterrestrial Creature Called on You?..152
Suggestions For Group Discussion 155
Notes 156

PREFACE

Getting Straight About the Bible is a studied and prayerful response to hundreds of persons who have asked me questions at lay retreats, church school classes, college classes, Bible conferences, and during numerous telephone calls. Some of these questions are clustered into four groups which form the four parts of this book.

Chapter 1, "How Did It All Begin" deals with questions concerned with the relationship between science and Christian faith. A clear distinction is drawn between the how and when of scientific discovery and the who and why of biblical faith. Thus science and faith are found to support one another, using the tools of study unique to their individual disciplines. I attempt to respond to such questions as: Did God create the world (universe)? How and when? How does biblical faith, especially Genesis 1, gear in with the findings of geology, biology, biochemistry, nuclear physics, and anthropology?

Chapter 2, "Do You Use or Abuse the Bible," deals with such questions as: What is the Bible? What is the *biblical* view of how the Bible was written? How were the books of the Bible selected? What are some abuses to be avoided as we study the Bible? What is the difference between eisegesis and exegesis of scripture? Can you illustrate how higher criticism really makes any difference in my study of the Bible?

Chapter 3, "What about the Rapture, the Second Coming, 666 . . . ," seeks to help persons read apocalyptic literature (such as Daniel and Revelation) with an understanding of this unique type of biblical literature. This chapter deals with questions such as: What is the origin of apocalyptic literature? How does it compare with the writings of prophets (such as Amos and Isaiah)? What is the meaning of the beasts (with many horns, crowns, blasphemous names, etc.)? What was the writer of Revelation seeking to say to his faithful flock in

11

A.D. 95? What is his real message for our time? What about Hal
Lindsey's, *et. al.*, interpretations about the rapture, the tribulation, the ten horned (and crowned) beast of Revelation 13, the
Second Coming? What is the Parousia of John's Gospel, and
when did John say the Presence would come to us?

Chapter 4, "Extraterrestrial Life and Intelligence," seeks to
help Christians who fear the possibilities of intelligent beings
existing on other planets—and their possible communication
with us earthlings. I deal with questions such as: does the
universe (or only earth) give evidence of God's mighty acts of
creation? What do outstanding scientists think about life and
possible intelligence on planets in interstellar space? What
scientists are trying to communicate with such beings? What
are some implications of NASA's projects? What is necessary
for a person to be designated as having been created in the
image of God? What qualities of kinship would "children of
God" hold in common? Would they experience truth, beauty,
goodness, faith? What is the relation of the Risen Lord to such
beings?

I would like to express appreciation to many persons who
have urged and encouraged me to write my convictions: Dr.
Raymond Bell (Professor of physics at Washington and Lee
College); to my wife who has so carefully read and reread the
manuscript and made scores of suggestions as well as doing
much of the typing; and to the hundreds of persons who have
heard my lectures and requested that I put my message in
written form.

I deeply appreciate the photos from NASA and the many
insights from former teachers of the Bible, professors and
writers of philosophy of religion, and students whom I taught
at Union College in Barbourville, Kentucky, and Hendrix College in Conway, Arkansas.

—HORACE R. WEAVER

HOW DID IT ALL BEGIN
(A Modern Study of Genesis 1)

INTRODUCTION

A few years ago I visited two communist countries: Russia and Yugoslavia. In both countries I was guided by two young adults: In Leningrad I was escorted personally through the anti-God museum (the former Cathedral of the Virgin of Kazan, now a museum of religion) by a young commanding officer of a USSR destroyer. In Belgrade I was escorted by a young man named Troska, a senior in the conservatory of music. Both of these young adults were deeply interested in the fact that I held a Ph.D. degree, had taught in a college for several years, and that I was also a Christian. The Russian communist tried to convince me that it was impossible to believe in God. He pointed out that he, with a class of some twenty students in the University of Moscow, had searched the heavens—seeking not only the locations of stars, but of any angels and for the throne of God! "But, Dr. Weaver," he said, "we never saw the throne of God!" His remark was very similar to that of Titov, the first Russian astronaut in space, who declared that while circling the earth, he too looked for the throne of God, but it was not in the heavens. Therefore there was no God!

I recall asking the Russian if he believed in only that which he could see, feel, taste, or smell. He shook his head affirmatively and said, "Da!" (yes). I asked him if he were not a scientist, to which he agreed. I asked him, perhaps impertinently, if he believed that an electron circled in orbits around the nucleus of its atom. He said quickly, "Of course!" I chided him a bit by asking: But have you seen an electron? Have you smelled one? Have you lifted one? Ever tasted one? "Of course not!" he replied. "But then, how can you believe in what you

13

have not seen or heard or smelled or tasted or lifted?" I then briefly stated my conviction that Christians were convinced by various reasons as well as by experiences of faith that God was as real as an electron. He shook his head and said, "I don't see how you can be intelligent and be a Christian at the same time!"

Troska, the musician at Belgrade, said almost the same thing to me. We had been talking about various interests that we had in common—I had studied some music in two conservatories in the United States, we both liked photography, and both of us enjoyed walking. I turned to Troska and asked: "Are you religious?" He laughed and replied, "Oh no, but my parents are." I prodded him a bit by asking why they were religious when he was not, to which he replied: "Oh . . . but they are only peasants!" I got the point, though he verbalized it for me: "I don't think a person can be intelligent and Christian at the same time. I'm studying at the university, so I don't believe in God."

Perhaps you might like to know the sequence that followed. Though mentally recognizing the difficulties with the deists' cosmological argument for belief in God, I took my watch off and showed it to him. I pointed out that my watch had two springs, one for the main spring of the watch and the other for a small alarm. I suggested that he hold an imaginary shoe box in his hand. He agreed, smiling. I then took out a small pocketknife and pretended to take the watch apart. I took off the hands, the numbers, the back, and took out the nineteen jewels and placed them in his box. I let the two springs fall free from their shells—and ceremoniously dropped them in the imaginary box in his hands. He laughed.

Then I paused to explain that my watch had a specially made balance shaft—made of an alloy of two metals so that the time would be accurate in hot and/or cold weather. So, I argued, I ought to melt down the two metals, separate them, and then drop them into his box. He agreed. I then asked him,

"Troska, how long would you have to shake this box before the watch would return to its original condition as you saw it first?" I was amused, then embarrassed, at his quick and hearty laughter. He raised his knee and hit it with his right hand, guaffawing so loudly that I thought perhaps he had been taught the weakness of this argument. But his words were: "Dr. Weaver, you could never get that watch together again by shaking the box. A watch is too complicated to make it by chance." I quickly responded, "We Christians feel this way about our world and our own bodies, too—especially when you think about the structure of our eyes (1,500 parts, I'm told), the uniqueness and complexity of the function of kidneys, liver, and heart, the remarkable way epithelial cells move from all parts of the body to come to the aid of a wound that has just been made in the body. If a watch requires a watchmaker, then how much more the human body requires a master designer!" I then suggested the complexity of interstellar space, the origin of matter (physical things), the complexity of the atomic and molecular world—these great systems also call for a master designer, a great mind. I shall never forget his words as we parted late that afternoon: "I begin to understand. I hope we can talk together some more." And I agreed too, for I wanted to tell him about the greatest person who ever lived, Jesus Christ, and help him see that no man (even his beloved Karl Marx or Lenin) has ever equaled, let alone surpassed him.

These two communists had asked me the same question: How can you be both a Christian and intelligent at the same time? Troska had tried to prove his point by stating that if you are a Christian, you have to believe that the world was made on April 23, at 10:00 A.M., 4004 B.C. (I had not heard of the exact hour before, but he informed me that it was given at the Scopes trial!) I assured him that I believed the world to have been created by God, and I accepted what scientists were telling us, namely, that our earth was about five billion years old. Troska made a final appeal: that one must choose between the Ages of Rock or the Rock of Ages. I assured him that the Bible was not a textbook in astronomy, biology, botany, nor geology. He looked stunned, for he had been taught that all Christians were ignorant, illiterate, unlettered persons. I also assured him that the Bible was a record of man's experience with God, that God was not only creator, but one who loved and sought to find fellowship with all persons of all countries.

In the years since, I have often thought of these experiences. I have also thought of high school students and college students in the USA who are troubled with problems similar to those Troska faced. How can we think about (harmonize) the story of creation in Genesis 1 with a scientific stance? Troska had listened intently and attentively as I explained my Christian understanding of the relationship of God to his world.

I believe it is important to grapple with the question: How can we relate the biblical record of creation with our current understanding of our physical and spiritual environment? Let me summarize the creative acts of God mentioned in Genesis 1 under four headings: light, the "heavens and the earth" (matter), "living things" (life), and mankind.

As we think about these four phrases from Genesis, let us go beyond what the writer of Genesis had in mind by asking what these words mean in the light of our present scientific understanding. For example, when we study about "the heavens and the earth" we will think in terms of our physical universe (matter)—our earth and its planetary system; this planetary system as a part of a galaxy of millions of galaxies.

We must not be bound to the ancient view that ours is a three-storied universe, with heavens above, hell below, and earth suspended in between, floating on water. In 1962 when John Glenn moved around our earth in his space craft it never occurred to him to look for God on his throne in heaven. This young Presbyterian scientist knew that God is not a physical God. So, the heavens must be interpreted in our day in the

light of modern cosmology and the sciences which deal with
space travel. We will still affirm "In the beginning God . . ."
But we will disagree with the biblical writers as to the size,
shape, and age of our earth and universe. In these matters
they were mistaken. The scientists tell us how the world was
made and approximately how long it took to make the earth
and to form living things (including man). The Bible tells us
who (that is, God) designed the processes by which all came
into being and tells us for what purpose he made them. God
was certainly the designer, planner, architect, creator! I re-
peat, the Bible does tell us that God made the heavens and the
earth, but it does not tell us how it was made. Scientists are
beginning to learn of God's methods and techniques. That is,
scientists are learning to "think God's thoughts after him."
God created all things that exist (physical and nonphysical), as
well as the laws that govern their relationships to each other.
Man only discovers, not creates, these laws. Again, man discovers God's thoughts as to how he made our world, and thus
man "thinks God's thoughts after him."

Let us consider now the first of the four acts of creation.

LET THERE BE LIGHT

"In the beginning God created the heavens and the earth.
The earth was without form and void, and darkness was upon
the face of the deep; and the Spirit of God was moving over the
face of the waters. And God said, 'Let there be light'; and there
was light! And God saw that the light was good" (Gen. 1-4).

The biblical writer of Genesis 1 lived in a period of history
very similar to our own. The theological and spiritual foundations were being threatened.

In the sixth century B.C., the most capable Jews of Judah had
been captured and were taken to Babylonia in exile. The
priests were forced to carry on their backs to a new land the
treasured and sacred instruments of Solomon's Temple. Here,

in Babylon, the sacred cups and books would be used pro-
fanely; the seven-branched candelabra would be desecrated.
So not only on their weary journey from Jerusalem to Babylon,
but while they labored as slaves they were taunted: "Where
now is thy God?" The Babylonians, who were also Semitic,
suggested that the Lord (Yahweh) was dead; the Jews should
worship the state god Marduk, who was not only stronger but
ruled the earth.

In this same sixth century, many thinkers were raising new
questions. In India the Buddha was denying the existence and
being of God. Buddha had sought God but could not find him.
Strangely, Buddha's followers idolized this atheist until he
(Buddha) was made a god. He is worshiped as a god to this
day.

In China, Confucius was raising questions about traditional
morality and offered a new ethics—one maxim being the
golden rule! The Persian kings who succeeded the Babylonians turned to a new faith. Cyrus the Great claimed that
Zoroaster offered the truth. Cyrus acknowledged two supreme
beings: Ahura Mazda (the good God) and Ahriman (the evil
God who would become known as the Satan, the devil, in
Jewish literature). The word for the good god "Mazda" meant
light. We Americans may be reminded of the Mazda electric
light bulb. It was during this Persian period that the Jewish
slaves affirmed their faith to be "a light to the nations."

Another great theological influence was astrology. First the
Babylonians, then the Persians (and later the Greeks and
Romans) adopted astrology as the best means of divining the
purposes of the gods for their personal and national life. An
astrologer was called a magus, the plural of which is *magi*.
They developed horoscopes based on the position of the
planets and the constellations in the sky. The signs and positions of the Zodiac determined their lives.

Then there were the early Greek philosophers of this period,
the Eliatic School of Philosophy at Miletus (on the western

shores of Asia Minor). They asked if there was anything that was permanent in life—Is there anything that never changes amidst all the constant flux of life? Is it water? Is it fire? Is it air? Parmenides suggested that Being never changes. The basis for all existence is Being.

Into this grand international debate about the death of God (such as Buddha's claim) or the existence of two supreme gods or the need for a new morality (Confucius) or the need for horoscopes due to the influence of divine planets or the search for that which never changes—into this vast theological discussion came the voice of the Jewish prophet, Isaiah of Babylon, who dealt with all the issues in his one claim of faith: "The grass withers, the flower fades; but the word of our God will stand for ever" (Isaiah 40:8).

Very simply, very beautifully, and very eloquently the prophet Isaiah made the claim: The Lord (Yahweh) is God: He alone rules the world; He alone is Creator. All else, including planets, are creatures of his making. He alone is the one Being that endures amidst all the changes of life.

The Lord God's method of creating all is based on his creative word: "And God said, 'Let there be light'; and there was light." (Genesis 1:3).

We affirm this biblical position. Before anything else existed, there was only God. "In the beginning God . . ." Our Judeo-Christian heritage affirms the view that God yearned for other beings like unto himself—creatures who could reason, experience beauty and truth, and be aware of and sensitive to each other. So God created a universe. His creative word brought into being many different energy systems—light, physical things, life, and thinking beings.

AND THERE WAS LIGHT

Genesis 1 affirms that God's first creative act was the creation of light. God simply said "Let there be light," and it was so. Not out of nothing *(ex nihilo)*, but out of his own being and nature God created light. Out of his own energizing will God brought forth an energy system, which includes what we call light.

Let us consider that which the biblical writer never dreamed as a possibility, namely: modern man's understanding of light. Light is a form of energy. It is not a physical thing. It has neither weight nor volume, but it does have motion, traveling at the speed of 186,286 miles per second. Now we know that when God created light, he also created the system within which light is but a small part. This energy, visible light, is part of the electromagnetic system of radiation. The electromagnetic spectrum spreads from the long wave lengths of radio to the short wave length of gamma rays.

About midway between either end of the electromagnetic spectrum is visible light; and it represents about 3 percent of the entire electromagnetic spectrum. Starting at the one end of the spectrum are the long wave lengths used in radio. Then moving toward visible light come shorter radio waves used for FM broadcasting and television. As the wave lengths get even shorter, we find the systems for radar and microwave relays. These lead to heat or infrared waves. Then comes visible light, of which Genesis 1 speaks. Visible light is made up of the rainbow colors from red to violet. The wave lengths that are shorter than violet are called ultraviolet. They cause suntans and are used in certain kinds of photography as well as for killing germs.

As the wave lengths get still shorter beyond the ultraviolet waves we get the familiar x-rays and gamma rays found in radioactive sources. Furthermore *mirabile dictu!* all these waves travel at the same speed—186,286 miles per second. What a designer God was and is!

Ezekiel and John of Revelation used the metaphor of the spectrum of light to portray the beauty of the heavenly assize. Their verbal painting showed the rainbow (the spectrum of

THE ELECTROMAGNETIC SPECTRUM

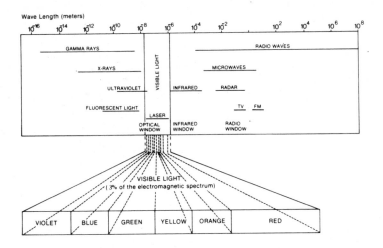

Figure 1

Every object (including each planet and/or sun) in the universe emits radiation in all the wave lengths of the above spectrum. Most radiation coming to our earth is absorbed by the earth's atmosphere. But waves in three portions of the spectrum penetrate the earth's atmosphere. These portions of the spectrum are called *windows* through which scientists can observe the universe. The three windows are: optical, infrared, and radio windows.

light) as the backdrop behind the throne of God (Ezekiel
1:26-28, Revelation 4:3-6).

Today scientists are using God's creative system of light in
wonderful ways. One of the most interesting uses of light is
the laser. Laser beams are made up of coherent light—*i.e.*, all
the waves in the beam are exactly of the same wave length, all
waves are exactly in phase with each other. With this unique
light an opthomologist can "weld" a fallen retina in the eye
back into place in a fraction of a second. It is bloodless
surgery! As a matter of fact, surgery is being improved by this
remarkable beam of light, God's first act of creation, for it
cauterizes the wound as it cuts, leaving no bleeding as with a
surgical knife. Laser is used also for dentistry, in treating skin
cancer, for cutting synthetic cloth for men's suits, for perfect
leveling of railroad tracks for fast moving trains. I have seen
the laser applied to a common brick which heats to 3,000
degrees celsius immediately! More significantly a laser beam
directed to a drop of a mixture of deuterium and flourine will
immediately produce heat equal to that of the sun—which is
the heat of an exploding hydrogen bomb. (Deuterium, a type
of hydrogen with atoms twice the mass of ordinary hydrogen,
is used in neuclear reactions and chemical investigations.) We
can produce all the heat we need to heat and cool our homes
and industries in the United States at a relatively low cost—
less than the cost of electricity produced by coal and gas! God's
system of light (via laser) was used to send messages from the
moon to earth. Metaphorically we think of God's greatest message sent to us in Jesus Christ, "the light of the world."

It seems apparent that God intended the entire energy system, the electromagnetic spectrum, to be used by thinking
beings. When God created light, he created an energy system
which can be used for tremendous good. As the scientist
discovers the laws and the multiplicity of uses of this kind of
energy, he is "thinking God's thoughts after him." None of
these modern uses of energy surprise God. After all, he created

them at the time he created light. "And God saw that it [light]
was good."

But there is a second system which God created and
through which God reveals himself as the supreme intelligent
being and because of which God has created intelligent beings
who will seek his truth in its many expressions.

GOD CREATED "THE HEAVENS AND THE EARTH"

"And God said, 'Let there be a firmament' . . . And God
called the firmament Heaven; . . . And God said, 'Let the
waters under the heavens be gathered together into one place,
and let the dry land appear.' And it was so. God called the dry
land Earth, and the waters that were gathered together he
called Seas. And God saw that it was good" (Genesis 1:6-10).
About five billion years ago God created the system we know
as "the heavens and the earth": matter.

Once again I suggest to the household of faith that in the
beginning was God, and God designed then created, not *ex
nihilo* (not out of nothing), but from his own energizing will.
He created the system we know as our physical universe.
God's creative word brought into being the atoms (such as
hydrogen, helium, and oxygen) of infinitesimally small structures. God designed the amazingly unique ways for atoms to
bind themselves to other atoms to form molecules and compounds and eventually the universe.

As modern man thinks of the heavens and the earth he
thinks of much more than the biblical writer dreamed. Modern man cannot hold to the cosmology of the biblical writer
who thought of his world as a three-story universe. Modern
man knows that the heavens and earth (matter) includes not
only our solar system but also our galaxy, the Milky Way; this
in turn is a part of billions of other galaxies in the universe.
Matter also includes the microscopic world of molecules and

the submicroscopic world of atoms with its electrons, protons, and neutrons. And of course matter includes the world known to our normal senses.

Philosophically speaking, our universe is not infinitely vast. Some scientists claim that our world is bounded, not un-bounded. If the universe is bounded, it is finite. And it had a time of origin, a time for its creation, too. Furthermore, new stars, new planets, new galaxies are continually being formed and sustained by law and orderly ways. In back of it all was and is the designing Father whose purposes are infinitely great—greater even than concern for just one of the millions of planets (earth) in our universe. God is still creatively at work throughout his universe.

Faith makes the claim that there is only one infinite and unbounded Being, and that is God. The universe is a creature, being created by God. Isaiah said it so beautifully for men of faith:

Have you not known? Have you not heard?
  Has it not been told you from the beginning?
Have you not understood from the foundations of the earth?
Have you not known? Have you not heard?
  The Lord is the everlasting God, the Creator of the ends of
  the earth.

Isaiah 40:21, 28

GOD'S DESIGN FOR MATTER

From our modern perspective, matter, though physical, is formed of infinitely small moving particles. A steel ball bearing seems very solid, yet it really is not! Millions of electrons move so fast around their many nuclei that we have the *impression of a hard, solid, stable ball*. For matter is not as it seems to be according to our senses. Actually God designed the steel ball bearing to be mostly empty space. Its weight and apparent hardness are due entirely to the remarkable union of atoms into molecules which cluster together. The billions of electrons in the steel ball bearing move so fast that we think the ball bearing in our hands is firm and hard.

Mentally, put your finger to the water faucet and get a drop of water. Look at the drop of water. Your finger is holding more than one hundred billion billion molecules of water. Each of these billions of molecules is made up of three atoms, two of hydrogen and one of oxygen.

Each of these atoms is providentially and wonderfully designed: the nucleus of the atom is made up of protons and neutrons (except hydrogen, which has no neutron). All other atoms have a nucleus of protons and neutrons around which electrons orbit. The protons are positively charged; the neutrons are neutral; electrons are negatively charged. An atom has the same number of electrons as there are protons, though the neutrons may vary in number.

A hydrogen atom has one proton (no neutron) in its nucleus and one electron that orbits the nucleus (see figure below). An oxygen atom has eight protons and eight neutrons in its nucleus, and eight electrons orbiting its nucleus. Note the two shells of an oxygen atom; the inner shell can hold only two electrons, the outer shell has six.

Let us see God's design for a molecule of water (H_2O):

When oxygen combines with hydrogen (to make a molecule of water) a reaction takes place: the electron in each hydrogen atom is drawn into the outer shell of the oxygen atom. This leaves the hydrogen atom without an (negatively charged) electron, and so leaves H atom positive (H^+). The oxygen atom

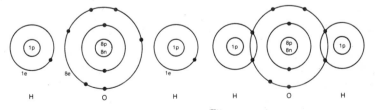

Figure 2

originally had eight electrons, but it gains one electron from each of the two hydrogen atoms, making ten electrons ($8 + 1 + 1 = 10$). The oxygen atom now has two more electrons (two additional negative charges). The H^+ and $O-$ (oxygen negative) are called ions.

The hydrogen atoms (positive charges) are attracted and held by the oxygen atom (negative charges). Thus molecules are atoms which are bonded together by sharing electrons (in their outer shells), being attracted to each other by their positive or negative charges. Hence we show H_2O: (H–O–H).

What a simple yet profound method God used in bonding atoms together to form molecules.

What a brilliant mind designed the submicroscopic world of atoms! This Mind (God) designed, purposed, and willed into being the structures of atoms and molecules (and solar systems) so that matter could be formed, and eventually living things, and finally man! In truth, as Isaiah said, "The heavens and the earth are full of the glory of God."

I think God must have had real pleasure as he designed and created matter. God so designed some elements (such as uranium and plutonium) that they could be separated (called fission): some atoms such as deuterium and tritium can fuse together (called fusion). In the process of fission and or fusion of atoms tremendous energy is developed—energy first used in the atomic bomb. Einstein gave us the formula: energy equals mass times the square of the speed of light, $E=mc^2$. Einstein said he received this formula by revelation from the cosmic mind (God)!

We of Judeo-Christian faith believe that God designed elements such as uranium with good, not evil purposes in mind—such as the use of nuclear reactors for fuel instead of burning coal or gas to produce electricity for man's use. Radioactive elements are being used in hundreds of creative ways in industry as well as agriculture and medicine, in research and treatment of diseases.

Einstein's formula $E=mc^2$ was developed, designed, and caused to function by God. (God revealed this physical law to Einstein, another Israelite lawgiver similar to Moses in the disciplines of ethics and theology.)

Earlier we observed the structure of an atom of hydrogen—one proton and one electron. This hydrogen atom is thought by many scientists to be the ancestral element from which other elements in the universe were formed in thermonuclear reactions. In their laboratories Urey and Miller discovered the [God's] way of creating the other elements. A strong radiant energy [light, from the electromagnetic spectrum] was directed on pure hydrogen, which eventually formed helium, and carbon was formed in the same way from helium. So many elements were formed.

The scientists discover, "read God's thoughts after him," *how* God made the elements. Faith tells us *who* designed and willed the system(s) into being. We may assume that the scientists' description is correct: Our sun and its larger planets condensed from the basic elements of hydrogen-helium-carbon some five billion years ago.

As we will note in the next section, God then made living things (self-organizing, self-directing, and self-reproducing). The environment which God made by his "slow" processes of creation included the one hundred elements, plus amino acids, sugars, carbohydrates (long chains of hydrogen and carbon), and the nucleotides of DNA. Various forms of life were developed in God's own timing (beginning ca. 3.2 billion years ago) through God's ordained method of "mutations."

We should always think theologically as well as scientifically, morally, and socially. The "eyes of faith" always see the divine designing activity of God behind God's universe. Yes, God created on both large and small scales. Scientists are now talking of miniaturized circuits for radio and television which will make use of molecules for circuitry. A molecule which has a high binding energy will be mated to a molecule of low binding energy. These two will act as conductors of electricity for very small radios.

Isaiah said it so succinctly: "Holy, Holy, Holy, Lord of Hosts. The whole earth [even its atoms, with their tremendous energy and power and their potential for good uses by man] is full of the Glory of God." True, "all things come from thee O Lord." And as we move from admiring a rose to analyzing it, we move from physical petals and stamina to molecules, to atoms, to neutrons, to electrons, to protons, to energy . . . to mathematical formulas which only minds can develop, beautiful formulas such as only the mind of God could make. Yes all things come from God. Truly, he is the alpha and the omega.

Recently I talked with a professor of nuclear physics. I told him of my religious experience as a college student while studying physics and calculus. At times I would get so excited I would place a small cross (†) on the margin of my page to express my conviction that only God could have brought that idea into being. The professor smiled and said, "I go to church, but my heart really sings when I'm at my lab."

He had isolated several particles of the nucleus of the atom. He said he truly worshiped and praised God at those times when God had revealed some of his infinite wisdom to him. Faith affirms that the scientist *discovers* that which God has built into the structure of the atom. As the scientist thinks God's thoughts after him and discovers his wonders, his heart is full of praise. We too honor, glorify, and give thanks for his creative providence.

Astronomers are as excited about the vast world of space as the nuclear physicists are about the minute world of the atom. Many astronomers are confident that some forms of life exist on thousands of planets. God is the Lord and Creator of this vastness of his universe, too.

Johannes Kepler, the founder of astronomy (died A.D. 1630), was moved to awe by the law and order he witnessed in the galaxies. He wrote in his first book *The Mysterium Cosmo-*

graphicum about his religious yearnings as a youth and young adult. "I wanted to become a theologian; for a long time I was restless, now, however [as a seasoned astronomer], observe how through my efforts God is being celebrated in astronomy." Kepler's observatory was an altar, where he worshiped the Creator of the universe. Kepler wrote that when he discovered the second law of planetary motion, he was in "sacred ecstacy." He was reading God's Word (laws) written in the structure of the stars.

The psalmist phrased it in words of ecstacy too:

> The heavens are telling the glory of God;
>   and the firmament proclaims his handiwork.
> Day unto day pours forth speech,
>   and night to night declares knowledge.
> There is no speech, nor are there words;
>   their voice is not heard;
> Yet their voice goes out through all the earth,
>   and their words to the end of the world (Psalm 19:1-4*a*).

CREATION OF LIVING BEINGS

God has revealed and reveals himself through his creation, not only through light and matter but also through life, as the intelligent being, the ground of all being. In Genesis 1:21 we read: "So God created ... every living creature that moves, with which the waters swarm, according to their kinds, and every winged bird according to its kind. And God saw that it was good." We read in Genesis 1:11-12 "And God said, 'Let the earth put forth vegetation, plants yielding seed, and fruit trees bearing fruit in which is their seed, each according to its kind, upon the earth.' And it was so.... And God saw that it was good."

We have considered the first two mighty acts of God in creation: the designing and creation of the electromagnetic system (which is symbolized in Genesis by the word light) and the energy system of matter (symbolized by "the heavens and the earth"). We turn now to the third energy system, which uses the other two energy systems but gives an entirely new dimension, namely: the world of living things—life.

People of faith readily claim that God, the loving Father of Jesus Christ was and is the who of creation. How did living things first come into being? How did protozoa (first life) appear in an environment of inorganic existence? How do you move from inert iron, copper, silver, gold, hydrogen, oxygen, and nitrogen to living beings that are self-propelling, self-directing, and self-reproducing? Can science help us understand how God may have worked in the designing and production of living things in his universe?

Molecular biologists are telling us that the secret to life is the DNA molecule. (DNA stands for deoxyribonucleic acid.) Many scientists consider it the most important discovery in the history of man. DNA is the key to the origin, maintenance, and continuity of life. DNA is not a chance creation of evolution or a "fortuitous concourse of events." God designed the structure and processes of the DNA.

Let us begin with our human bodies. Almost every cell in the body (the brain is the exception) has a DNA molecule in its nucleus. It has been estimated that each of us has about sixty-billion DNA molecules, each exactly alike. Each of the sixty billion DNA molecules is a type of submicroscopic computer—but more, for it is alive! A DNA molecule is visible only under an electron microscope. These invisible computers are formed by a remarkable interplay of proteins and amino acids and elements such as oxygen, nitrogen, hydrogen, sugar, and phosphates.

God has designed human life so that each and every one of the sixty billion computers (DNA) in our bodies carry identically the same genetic code for our individual lives. At the union of sperm and ovum a new DNA molecule is formed and with it a totally new set of genes and chromosomes. A DNA molecule may be thought of as a long strand or sequence of hundreds of genes. At conception the DNA molecule determined the color of your hair, the color of your eyes, the shape of your nose, your ears, your fingers, and your toes. Your hereditary traits were coded into the DNA so that every feature you would have when you become an adult was coded into those submicroscopic computers. The DNA code also carries undesirable information about possible color blindness, proneness to deafness and to certain diseases (such as sickle cell anemia and hemophilia). For example, my left eye has a colaboma, a "cat eye"; this means the pupil is enlarged vertically. My father and grandfather had a colaboma, too. So at conception, my DNA was coded for colaboma. And every one of my sixty billion DNA molecules in every cell of my body (except the brain cells) has that same "colaboma" information coded into it.

Dr. Beadle, Nobel Prize winner in the area of molecular biology, has stated that each of these sixty billion DNA molecules in our bodies has information coded into the spiral-like chain that, if printed, would fill one thousand volumes of the *Encyclopedia Britannica*. Remember: each of these miniaturized computers are so small they are invisible except with an electron microscope, yet each contains enough information to fill one thousand volumes! You carry in your body the equivalent of sixty trillion (sixty billion times one thousand) volumes of built-in information! Not to believe in God as the source of our physical and living being calls for more credulity than I could possibly muster.

Let us look at the DNA molecule more closely, for it tells us how God brought life into being—how he took inorganic matter (amino acids, nitrogen, carbon, hydrogen, oxygen, sugar, and phosphate), designed and created it to move, grow, reproduce, propel and guide itself, swim, walk, or fly, and finally made a being with the potential to experience intelligent decisions, moral choice, and to fellowship with the Holy.

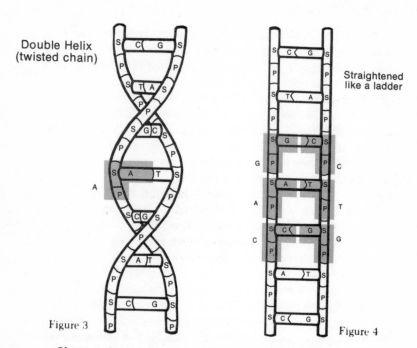

Double Helix (twisted chain)

Straightened like a ladder

Figure 3

Figure 4

Observe in figure 3 that the verticle (uprights) of the chain are formed of two kinds of molecules (sugar "S", and phosphate "P"), and that they always alternate: S-P-S-P-S, etc. Observe in figure 4 that the sugar (S) molecule is bonded in each rung of the ladder to one of four letters: A, C, T, G. So, in the rungs of the ladder you would find: S-G or G-S; or S-A or A-S; S-C or C-S; or S-T or T-S. In figures 3 and 4 look for a combination like S-A. These three molecules (A, S, P) in the ladder form the letter A. Adjacent to the letter A must be the letter T which looks like T-S. The letters A and T fit together: S-A T-S and form one rung of the ladder (S-A, T-S), and also part of the verticle chain! The letter A is known as an adenine nucleotide; T is a thymine nucleotide; C, a cytocine nucleotide; and G is a guanine nucleotide.

In figure 4 in the left verticle (upright) of the chain are three letters: G, A, C. These three letters form one word (GAC) or codon. The codon GAC is one of the sixty-four words in God's language of life! Note that each rung of the ladder is a bonding of A to T or T to A; C to G or G to C. These letters are like pieces of a jigsaw puzzle and will fit only in this way. It's a God ordained rule!

How can you think about this marvel, the DNA? Think of a long chain ladder, slightly twisted, with narrow rungs between the vertical chains. A casual glance at figures 3 and 4 illustrates what the twisted chain (the double helix) of the DNA molecule looks like.

Yes, God created life by way of the DNA. There are sixty-four three-letter words in the language of life. All living things, a dandelion, rose, gnat, squirrel, and persons are formed from these sixty-four words (codons). These codons are bonded together in such a mathematical, biochemical, and truly aesthetic way that we marvel at the divine ingenuity which designed and created this energy system of life. The DNA uses the complicated three-letter words (like GAC) to code (write in) the hereditary traits of various species of plants and animals. It is through changes in the organizational pattern of the codons that God planned for mutations in species to take place!

Figure 5

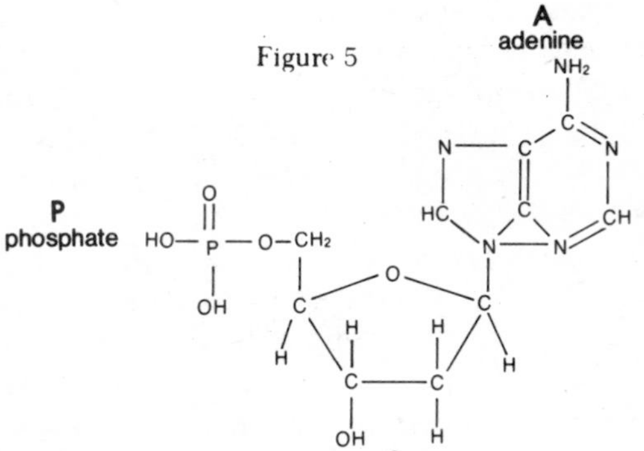

figure 5 A diagram of the letter A: (adenine nucleotide)
The chemical structure of the letter "A" (adenine nucleotide) is formed from three molecules: A (adenine), S (sugar) and P (a phosphate). Of course A would be three dimensional, with electrons whirling around the nucleus of each of the atoms; and atoms and molecules being bonded together via the electrons in the outer shells of each of the atoms noted above in figure 5.

Take a pencil and write down the following facts and marvel at the brilliance of the divine intelligence in creating the energy system of life: In the left hand corner of your page write sixty billion cells, which is the number of DNA molecules you have in your body. Under that write one cell, which has eight million genes; then write one gene, which generally has a sequence of one thousand bases; then under bases write: one base has a three-letter word drawn from sixty-four possible words.

60,000,000,000 cells
    1 cell: 8,000,000 genes
        1 gene: 1,000 bases (letters A, T, C, G)
           1 base: one letter (as "A-nucleotide")
              with its structure of 3 molecules

Think of the possible combinations above! Does that make your imagination swim? It does mine! We believe that only the divine being could design and order into being and maintain such a miniaturized system. Remember, each of these sixty billion cells carries the same coded information. So that, according to where the cell is located (in the eye, nose, liver, ears, heart, heel) the coded information is used according to the need of the organ where it is located. For example: If your eye needs a certain enzyme by which to allow the synthesis of the light-sensitive chemicals that make vision possible, the code in the DNA sends messages to attend to these needs. What a marvel of computer-engineering!

THE MIRACLE OF REPRODUCTION

God created laws and processes by which living things are reproduced. At certain times the long ladder-like DNA splits lengthwise. Individual bases (letters A C T G), which are in the cytoplasm of the cell, are drawn into the nucleus to join with the "open" DNA. A complement is formed. This complement is the messenger RNA (mRNA) which goes into the cytoplasm to be read by ribosomes which then produce needed protein. The DNA molecule stays in the nucleus and is dupli- cated during cell division and the process starts all over again—so that every new cell carries exactly the same infor- mation as the original DNA molecule.

The scriptures of Genesis states: In the beginning God formed swarms of living things in the waters. How beautifully this describes the beginning of life as molecular biology now describes it. John's Gospel adds another dimension: "In the beginning was the Word." Combining Genesis 1:1 and John 1:1, I like to think that this creative Word "hovered over" inorganic matter of earth and superimposed upon inorganic matter the sixty-four words which brought life into being. Protozoa was born! First life came into being. And God said let there be living things, and God said it is good. Thus, the flora and fauna of earth and the universe came into being.

One of the marvels of all this is the universalism inherent in the DNA, especially the sixty-four codons. Bacteria, amoeba, all plants and animals, and man have precisely these very same words of life. This would be true of life anywhere in our universe! All living things hold much in common—our God-given DNA and its processes. It all goes back to the Fatherhood of God (Creator-Father) who willed us all into being. A new respect for life seems apparent, doesn't it? St. Francis may have been close to the truth when he prayed for sister deer and brother plants.

All the above miniaturized world seems to be impossible. It helps me a bit to recall that I carried a one-page Bible in my wallet—the card was a "fish," a specially printed card with miniaturized printing of 848 pages of the Bible. The pages of this Bible were so small that a high powered light microscope was needed to read the pages. But this Bible with all its 848 pages reproduced on one small (2″ x 3″) card, is nothing in comparison to the smallness of the DNA molecule which cannot be seen except through an electron microscope.

I can almost hear Troska, my communist guide, saying: "I begin to see why you believe in God."

But, I have been asked: How long did it take life to move from protozoa to man? Molecular biologists think that the DNA came into being (was *created* as I phrase it) about 3.2 billion years ago. The creative word of God designed living things so that mutations would produce different species. Light and radiation from the electromagnetic system played a part in God's development of different species.

God's method of creation of plants and animals apparently was from the simple to the complex and on to ever more complex. This process is referred to as evolution. We would point out that *evolution did not design nor create the species*. God, who designed the process called evolution, is the Creator. Laws did not create anything. Laws don't rule the universe. God—who made the laws—rules! These processes are described but not created by scientists. The processes, like the things of inorganic life, are creatures and are God-made. There is only one Creator, but millions of creatures. These creatures include radiation (as found in the electromagnetic spectrum), elements (such as iron, copper, hydrogen and oxygen), living things (produced by God's use of DNA), plants, animals and fish, and finally millions of years later human beings. Each and all are totally dependent on God, not only for their creation, but for their maintenance and sustenance now.

Not only the heavens declare the glory of God, but so do all his creatures, each of which cries out: Holy, Holy, Holy, Lord God of Hosts; the earth is full of thy glory.

CREATED IN HIS IMAGE

Then God said, "Let us make man in our image, after our likeness; and let them have dominion over the fish of the sea, and over the birds of the air, and over the cattle, and over all the earth, and over every creeping thing that creeps upon the earth." So God created him in his own image, in the image of God he created him; . . . And God saw everything that he had made, and behold, it was very good (Genesis 1:26-27, 31).

After God had made the energy systems of the electromagnetic spectrum, matter, and living beings, then God made another different energy system. This time it was an energy system which again used the previous systems, but added a new dimension: the spiritual. God created mankind with the potential of spiritual experiences.

The account of creation of man in Genesis 1 differs from the account of creation found in Genesis 2:4b-24. In the second account God took the dust of the earth (Adamah) and made from mother earth (Adamah) a man (Adam). In Genesis 1 we have a much later and more sophisticated account of creation. In fact chapter 1 corrects the view of chapter 2 in at least two points. First, God did not take dust from the ground and mold it into a man, then breathe breath of life into the dust. Rather, God created as he had created all other energy systems: the great creative God created by simply willing it into existence. God had said: "Let there be light," and there was light; God had said: "Let there be the heavens and the earth," and it was so. God had said: "Let there be living things," and it was so. Now God said: Let there be human beings, and it was so. Secondly, chapter 1 states that God did not create a man named Adam as the first human being; rather God made mankind. The Hebrew word used in 1:26 is *Adam,* which is a generic word meaning mankind (human beings). When a specific man named Adam is referred to, the article "the" is placed in front of the noun, and it becomes Haadam ("the man," *i.e.,* Adam, a name of a man).

As a youth and young adult I often wondered where Cain, having been exiled from Eden for killing his brother, found a wife who bore him a son named Enoch. I recall thinking that since God had made only Adam and Eve, and they had two sons, one being killed by Cain, that possibly Cain married a sister. But that wasn't supported by the biblical text. So I wondered where Cain did find a woman. Was Eve the only woman? The answer of course is that God made mankind. Cain was forced out of the family circle for murder and eventually found a woman of another people (possibly another race) "east of Eden."

Let us observe once again that God's mighty acts of creation moved through the creative processes of development from the simple to the complex to ever greater complexity. Human beings were created after God's magnificently designed DNA molecule had produced thousands of forms of life: God's brilliant creation of the DNA brought all kinds of flora and fauna to his universe and our earth. Mankind was a high point of God's creative action.

GOD'S MIGHTY ACTS IN CREATION OF LIFE

Mankind appeared first, as scientists are telling us, in the form of *homo erectus*. The date given for Adam (mankind) is 1,300,000 years ago. Where does this date fit in with other living things? Let me suggest several interesting "firsts" with dates. I suggest these because many school children learn these same dates, but do not see them as related to Christian faith. The following list suggests the continuing creative acts of God in the history of our earth and living things.

5,000,000,000 years ago: God created the earth and the moon
4,000,000,000: God created the sea
3,200,000,000: God willed into being the DNA (with its sixty-four words of three letters each): the beginning of life—algae and bacteria appear on the water.
600,000,000: fish and invertebrate animals

200,000,000: birds are created
 40,000,000: monkeys and apes
  1,300,000: *Homo erectus*, the first man ("Adam" of Genesis 1) via God's use of DNA in ever more complex forms. (Some scientists set the date: 2,000,000.)
    100,000: Neanderthal man in Europe
     35,000: Cro-Magnon man in Europe; North and South America populated by Asian hunters.
  9,000 B.C.: Jericho (of Old Testament fame) settled
  7,300 B.C.: Man learns to cultivate wheat and barley, in Near East
  6,000 B.C.: Cattle are domesticated
  3,500 B.C.: The wheel is invented in Sumer (Mesopotamia); Man learns to write— drawing-pictures; Copper age
  3,000 B.C.: Bronze age
  2,600 B.C.: Pyramids of Egypt built; Gilgamesh epic (Sumer)
  2,400 B.C.: Stonehenge
  2,000 B.C.: Eskimo culture
  1,400 B.C.: Iron age in Near East; (1200 B.C. in Palestine)
  1,250 B.C.: Moses introduces Monotheism and Ten Commandments.[1]

We return to the biblical phrase: "God created man in his own image." What does that mean? First, let us remind ourselves that God is Spirit, not having any physical characteristics whatsoever—no hands, no feet, no body. The writer of Genesis 1 knew that God was Spirit. What did he mean when he wrote man is created in the image of God? Since God is nonphysical, but Spirit, our writer was referring to spiritual categories. In our terms these categories, which man potentially holds in common with God, are in the disciplines of ethics, aesthetics, intelligence, and holiness.

Man was created with the potential for learning to reason, to enjoy beauty, to prefer truth and fellowship with God and persons. But man can refuse to recognize these God-given potentialities; he may learn about each of them and refuse to live by them, preferring immorality, ugliness, falsehood, and unrelatedness to God and persons. Man can also choose to fulfill his potentials in all these areas, until his life reflects actions based on a high ethical code, a love for the beautiful in life, a passion for truth in every discipline of life, and a humble walk with his Creator, Judge, Redeemer, and Father. Man can so walk with God in the fulfillment of God's dream for persons that others can see that God's Spirit is reflected in his life—in truth they are sons and daughters of the living God. Such persons find meaning and purpose in life. Their meaning is found in awareness of the presence of God (Immanuel) and in fulfilling their lives as God had dreamed when he originally planned for their existence.

I have been talking about the spiritual experiences of persons. By spiritual I mean those experiences which are not produced by the physical body—experiences such as truth, love, justice, mercy, kindness, good will, beauty. These are experiences that are beyond the processes of DNA or of molecular or atomic processes. These spiritual experiences must be willed by persons. Persons are not loving, just, merciful, thoughtful merely through being born a human being. Persons are born with the potential for becoming spiritually minded beings or to live the life of the animal. Many persons choose to live like animals, and their actions often identify them as being on the level of the alley cat or dog.

A great biologist has said that the only difference between Jesus and Judas was their pituitary glands. Judas' pituitary glands moved him to deny Jesus; while Jesus' pituitary glands moved him to be loyal to God at all costs—even to dying on the cross. I deny this kind of ethical and spiritual nonsense. Persons choose, as I am confident Jesus and Judas chose, between possible alternatives. Luke, in his Gospel, states this fact so succinctly: "Judas became a traitor." One is not born a traitor. One's choices in life inevitably lead one to set a character which determines actions. But personalities can be changed. This is the point of rebirth. God has made it possible for a morally filthy person to become clean, for an ignorant man to become intelligent, for a blasphemous person to love God. Man is potentially a spirit being; his potential is different from that of any other creature on earth.

I would like to add that you cannot reproduce a St. Francis by taking drugs. You may experience a similar experience by way of drugs, but this is not an authentic religious experience. You don't make a saint out of a sinner by pumping heroin or some other chemical into his blood stream. Normal persons become saints because of choices which fulfill God's dream for all persons—choices of moral life, goodness, and holiness.

It is not by accident that thousands of persons who love beauty (as found in music, arts, drama) have found God in their experiences of beauty. It is not by accident that thousands of persons who love truth (as scientists in search of basic laws which undergird our world; as persons in other intellectual disciplines who yearn for more knowledge) find God in the process. So it is also in the search for moral life as it is related to justice, not only for our own lives but for persons of all races, classes, creeds, and physiognomy. This dream of God was fulfilled in Jesus Christ. The Risen Lord calls us to fulfill his purposes for man (Isaiah 61:1-4; Luke 4). A life of justice, mercy, compassion, good will toward all persons often leads to a sense of Immanuel! And an assurance of at-onement with God in his redemptive work in this world.

PERSON'S RESPONSES IN FAITH AND LOVE

Try to imagine God's pleasure in his sensitivity to those persons who developed their spiritual potential—such as the poet-psalmist who sang: "The heavens declare the glory of God and the firmament showeth his handiwork." And God's appreciation of the entomologist, Jean Henri Fabre, who, after having studied the process of cross-pollination of flowers by insects, ecstaticly and reverently declared: "Before these mysteries of life reason bows and abandons itself to adoration of the author of these miracles." I also think God enjoyed and highly valued the remarks of a latter-day Israelite, the scientist Albert Einstein, who discovered the remarkable formula by which God "permits" energy to change to matter and matter to change back to energy: $E = mc^2$. Einstein said:

> The most beautiful and profound emotion we can experience is the sensation of the mystical. It is the sower of all true science. He to whom this emotion is a stranger, who can no longer wonder and stand rapt in awe, is as good as dead. To know that what is impenetrable to us really exists, manifesting itself as the highest wisdom and the most radiant beauty which our dull faculties can comprehend only in their most primitive forms—this knowledge, this feeling is at the center of true religions.

God appreciated this statement because it is a response of faith and love. Einstein was developing the potential of his spiritual life—intellect, aesthetic, moral, religious. It is inspiring to know that great scientists "cast their golden crowns upon the glassy sea."

We affirm with Isaiah: "Holy, Holy, Holy, is the Lord of Hosts. The whole earth is full of thy glory." We can affirm this in ways never dreamed of by Isaiah. *All* existence is a medium of revelation—the whole earth reveals the glory of God. Scientists and religious persons can walk arm in arm on this road of faith-experience.

My mind is always refreshed by the fact that the farther back the scientist goes, the farther he pushes back to the mind that originally created those mental constructs—the mind of God! The ultimate source and fount of being is God.

Out of man's long search to fulfill the built-in "image of

God," mankind has developed language, writing, literature, law, buildings, cities, government, concern for all persons. As human beings respond to their fullest God-given [and God-coded!] potentials we approach the Kingdom of God—which was and is God's dream for mankind.

To fulfill the "image of God" in a person's life, one needs to include all the spiritual values we have noted in the disciplines of ethics, aesthetics, intellectual studies, and faith. If a person omits any one of these areas in his experience, he is lopsided and incomplete. He distorts the image of God. A few years ago Bruno Bettleheim raised the question of how a Nazi doctor could be so cautious about antiseptic procedures in helping a Jewish mother give birth to her child, sterilizing the instruments, and carefully sterilizing the cut umbilical cord when only a half hour later he ordered the mother and baby to be burned in a crematorium. Dr. Bettleheim asks: How can a physician reconcile his role as a healer with inhuman acts that made the doctor (Dr. Mengele) do this to the mother and child? The answer was that Dr. Mengele took great pride in his professional skills, regardless of the function they served. How lopsided it is to be successful in the search for truth, but unconcerned about moral life and social action!

Genesis 1 also states that persons are created to have dominion over all the earth. This has been interpreted to mean that a person can do as he or she pleases with God's resources in and on the earth. Our abuse of nature has led us to a terrible situation and a frightening future for our children. The oil reserves of this small planet earth may last only a few decades—possibly depleted by A.D. 2010 and coal depleted by A.D. 2320. Our oxygen supply is being decimated by various nations hauling their garbage into the oceans where it is dumped, destroying well over half the plankton that grows in the waters of the ocean. Yet our earth receives 85 percent of our oxygen supply from the plankton that grows in the oceans.

Our brutal raping of the land, the oceans, and the minerals

within the earth are leading us to the edge of catastrophe. Famine stalks countless nations, with tens of thousands dying from starvation. Our population of the planet earth is 4,000,000,000 persons today, but it will be 7,000,000,000 by the end of this century. How do we feed so many mouths when there isn't enough food even now for all persons? These questions call for persons to begin to exercise their potential as human beings, to think ethically (hopefully from the perspective of the life and teachings of Jesus) about the needs of people around the world and our part in meeting their varied needs, to think aesthetically, intellectually, and express our faith in God's good providence and dream for mankind.

Lastly, I want to suggest that in and through Jesus Christ, God has revealed the goal of his creation for mankind. God's will and purpose in creation was the development of persons who would respond in faith and love to his presence and will to the extent that they, through the influence and saving power of Jesus, would be Christ-like persons. The purpose of creation is marred and distorted by man's alienation from God. The consequent sins of hate, greed, selfishness, and unconcern have estranged man from man too. The image of God has been so distorted that man cannot see the beatific vision of what he was made to be.

In Jesus the image of God in human beings has been restored, and we see the clear purpose of God's creation of and for persons. Humanity has the option of choosing between Christ-likeness or the demonic. And indeed every person does choose between them. We are either Christ-possessed people or demon-possessed people. But God's purposes were and are that men might choose the Christ-like way, find their new being in him, and thus find abundant life.

But time is actually running short on this biosphere called earth. Man is facing some ultimate decisions about, not only God, but about the future of this planet. The decision to choose to live in the image of God is not a light one. It is a decision that faces all mankind; and in that decision rests the future of our earth. That future cannot avoid the person in whom Paul saw the glory of God reflected in his face, life, death, resurrection, and presence as the living Lord of his life.

SUGGESTIONS FOR GROUP DISCUSSION

1. Let persons in the group discuss the communist's claim that you cannot be both Christian and intelligent. The problem is: What is the function of reason in matters of faith? Should or can faith and reason support one another?

2. Why is it important to distinguish between the how and when of science and the who and why of biblical faith? Ask someone to apply these perspectives to Moses' experience at the crossing of the Red Sea (Exod. 14:12).

3. Set aside a period of time for witnessing by various individuals when they have been in a "religious ecstacy" (to use Kepler's phrase) as they thought God's thoughts after him—perhaps in music, art, or medicine; at work in a lab; in one of the descriptive sciences; physics, biochemistry, botany; at special moments as a parent.

4. Let two parents discuss why it is important for boys and girls to be able to relate God's mighty acts of creation to what they are being taught in geology, biology, ancient history, etc.

5. If God is Spirit, what does it mean to be made in the image of God? Let each person turn to two other persons and tell them why he or she believes they are in the image of God. Are there some decisions that each person might make that would help them more clearly reflect this image of God in their lives? Be specific—confess your sins, and renew your spirit! What is God's goal for each and every human life?

NOTES

[1]*The First Men,* (New York: Time-Life Books, 1973), pp. 148-49.

DO YOU USE OR ABUSE THE BIBLE

(Letting God Speak Through Its Pages)

EFFECT OF ATTITUDES

Dr. Edgar Sheffield Brightman was considered one of the most brilliant philosophers of the past generation. One day, during a class session, I heard a student ask the learned man this question, "If you had to undergo some kind of forced isolation and you were permitted to choose only two books from your library, which two would you choose?" Now Dr. Brightman had invested thousands of dollars in books. I understand that he and his family had agreed that instead of owning cars they would own books. So Dr. Brightman had a wonderful library in his study. I recall how quickly Dr. Brightman responded to the question with these words: "I would choose the writings of Plato and the Bible."

Dr. Brightman loved his Bible. He used it daily. But he brought his best thinking to his reading of scriptures. One of the first books written by this philosopher was on the sources of the Hexeteuch—a study of the various traditions and documents from which the first six books of the Old Testament were compiled. His attitude toward the Bible, which included a deep respect and love for the scriptures, determined his readiness to let God speak through its pages. There can be no question but that he heard God's voice many times.

The attitudes which we bring to the Bible, even though we truly honor God and are sincere about his Word, may be a block between us and God's Word. Our attitudes determine whether we use or abuse scripture. I would like to illustrate what I mean.

A few years ago I attended a Christian worship service in an Eastern Orthodox cathedral in Belgrade, Yugoslavia. The building was rectangular and had seats placed only in one row at the back of each of three walls. There were several hundred persons present, though only a few score were seated. (I was one of them.) The congregation played the part of spectators for the most part. During the two-and-a-half-hour service the priests sang and celebrated the mass. There were probably a dozen priests in the apse, behind the raredos—which looked like a lovely lattice work in mahogany. They moved continually around the altar celebrating the eucharist. The congregation was aware of what was going on, ecclesiastically, though they did not participate.

I recall how beautiful one of their priestly songs was—we had sung it in our college choir on tours a number of times. It was "Hospodi Pomilui" (Lord God have mercy). The all-male choir of priests sang it with rare beauty, with the appropriate diminuendos and crescendos that made you feel that the roof of the cathedral had somehow been removed and you were a participant in the heavenly assize. They loved the Lord. Remember that Yugoslavia is a communist land. As such those who profess Christ are not permitted to assume leadership roles as managers of factories or farms; nor are they elected to attend universities. Why should they? As my guide Troska had said: "You cannot be both intelligent and Christian at the same time."

During the last half hour of the service I witnessed a most unusual event. The priests left the apse, the inner holy of holies where they had been celebrating the mass, and entered the nave where the congregation of several hundred had been standing for over two hours. The processional was led by a tall, handsome, black-bearded patriarch, dressed in black, with a large and beautiful silver crucifix hanging from a chain around his neck. He proudly carried an object on a plush scarlet pillow, holding it at arms length from his body. It was a large Bible. It was inlaid with precious jewels—sapphires, emeralds, amethysts, sardius, sardonyx, jasper, diamonds, and the other jewels of the breastplate worn by the priests of ancient Israel.

The patriarch carried the Bible to various areas among the congregation. The members of the faith reached out to touch the Bible with their handkerchiefs as he walked by. I saw them kissing their "holy" handkerchiefs, make the sign of the cross over their foreheads and hearts, then lovingly fold the handkerchiefs and place them carefully in pocket books or clothing. These Christians, surrounded by a hostile philosophy of communism, loved their Bible. There was no doubt about it. They treasured it and revered it highly. Yet, strangely, they never opened that precious book and read from the sacred scriptures during the entire morning. Their attitude was one of reverence and awe—yet they never listened to its message.

This kind of reverence becomes idolatry. The congregation revered their sacred object to the point where their attitude became a block to letting the message of God speak through the pages to them for their day.

We American Protestants all too easily become idolatrous toward the Bible too. The Protestant reformation lifted the Bible to the place of authority for faith and practice. In doing so we honored the Bible above all other claims of authority— such as church traditions, pronouncements, creeds, papal bulls. Translations were made from the Greek, Hebrew, and Aramaic so that every man could read the Bible for himself. This was a great boon for Western civilization.

Yet this attitude of honor for the greatest authority of our faith has brought the charge of idolatry against us too. We have read our Bibles in ways that have abused it rather than used it as a means of hearing God speak to us in clear and certain words. We have searched for eternal principles, laws, or legalistic requirements rather than for God.

Furthermore, we have refused to accept biblical statements about its origin—how it was written, how it became authoritative, in what ways it is authoritative today. We are, as are the Christians in Belgrade, sometimes idolatrous with the Bible. It often lies in a conspicuous place—often on an end table by the bed—but is hardly ever opened for concentrated study. We revere it, lovingly dust it, feel the nostalgic sacredness of it. We often misuse or abuse the Bible by the attitudes we bring to it.

I recall visiting a church in Moscow. It was called "Christ Behind the Iron Bars." At the top of the steps, before the main entrance to the church was a statue of Jesus. But there were tall iron bars set up to keep the people from going up the steps to the statue of Jesus. Entrance to the church was by a smaller side door. As I looked at the statue of Christ behind the iron bars I wanted to tear down the iron bars to release the Christ, that he could mingle with humanity as was his custom in the days of his flesh. But the church of 1918 and earlier thought that Jesus was the aloof one, the stern one of judgment as so many of the icons portray him. My resentment of this misinterpretation of Jesus was mitigated somewhat as I thought of how we do this with our Bibles. Sometimes we, too, imprison the Word so that it cannot enter the world and release its message. We too build walls around the Bible that keep the Word carefully guarded, protected, and imprisoned. The Word can't get out and become incarnate among us.

Let us look at those attitudes that falsely honor and thereby dishonor the Bible by making it too sacred for daily use or by attitudes that force the Word of God into a frame of reference (a prison with iron bars, if you will) in which it was never intended to be placed. Let us learn how to use, not abuse, the Bible.

WHAT IS THE BIBLE?

At the close of World War II, thousands of displaced Russians (captives of Germany's invasion of Russia) were freed by our military forces. These captives of war had been forced to work as slaves throughout the Reich. I was in the 1131st

Engineer Combat Group who freed about twenty of these Russian persons, all of them girls between twenty and twenty-one years of age.

I recall our first Sunday service in the parlor of Baron Von Thysson's manor, where these girls had labored for five years. As our headquarter's company met for service and were singing the first hymn, these twenty young women came in and sat in the back of the room. They sang and prayed at the appropriate times in the service. At the close of the service, after the men had left the room, the spokesman for the group asked if I would hold prayer services for them and if I would preach to them. These Russian girls were the most unusual group I had ever met. All were Christians. For five years they had met each evening before retiring from a very hard day's work. They met to quote from memory the Scripture passages which they had learned from their family devotions in childhood or church school in Russia. They sang their hymns and offered prayers each night during their five years of virtual slavery.

These girls asked me to preach to them. I wondered what they would want to hear—these Christian young people who had been so wonderfully loyal to their Lord during these years of oppression. So I asked them: What would you like for me to speak to you about? They huddled together as though they were a team ready to make strategic plans in a football game. They sat down, and Lydia Postuwaska, whose name I shall never forget, said: "Tell us about God." I thought: What can a person such as I tell this group of loyal Christian young people? I concluded: The essence of the Scriptures and of the life of Jesus is that God loves us. So I told them that. When I couldn't think of the right word I cradled my arms and rocked them and said in German: "As a mother loves her baby, so God loves you." I never realized before so clearly how much people want to hear the Word of the loving God.

Within a year about fifteen of these girls had died from

tuberculosis. But their faces of sincerity and faith are etched in my memory. I shall never forget the next meeting I had with them, when they asked if I would get them a Bible printed in Russian. I agreed to try. And try I did. I contacted all the DP (displaced persons) camps around Dusseldorf. I went to dormitories and asked: *"Haben Sie ein Bibel?"* And they would look at each other quizzically, and ask: "Was ist ein Bibel?" (What is a Bible?) I contacted over 10,000 Russians and never found a single copy for these girls. I did give each of them a New Testament in English, which they treasured and from which they learned to speak in English during the next few weeks and months.

Well, what is a Bible? How would you describe the Bible to one who had never heard of it? Suppose some members of your community had never heard of a Bible, and you gave them the New English Bible. What would you say about it? (Try this out sometime—describe your Bible!) You might offer some statistics such as: it weighs two pounds, it is 6″ x 7″ x 1″. You could show them the table of contents: Sixty-six books within its covers, indeed a veritable library. You might point out that the book has two major sections called the Old Testament and the New Testament. You might point out that the sixty-six books are of different length and style. Each is a different type of literature—some historical, others poems (Judges 5, the Psalms); some are letters (Romans, Corinthians, Philemon); some are laws (Leviticus, Exodus 20-23); some books are short novels (Jonah and Ruth); and apocalypse (Daniel 2, 7-12; Revelation); some are gospels (Matthew, Mark, Luke, John), and so forth. Then you might explain that these books were written in different times, places and under varying conditions. In fact, they were written over a period of thirteen hundred years, during the rule of many different nations. The books were each written in one of three languages: Hebrew, Aramaic, or Greek.

In responding to the question "What is the Bible," statistical and historical statements are inadequate. The Bible is not understood until we see it in relationship to both man and God. The literature of the Bible developed out of the experiences of persons in their encounter with God. Biblical literature is a record of God's search for man and man's search for and response to God. There are times when a person wants to hear an authentic word from God.

I recall vividly an experience with my father-in-law three days before he died. He had been a hard working man, a sheetmetal worker by trade. He sometimes put on an exterior of being rough, but underneath there was a wonderful softness, concern, and love. We were visiting with him in his last few hours. He turned to me as we started to leave and said: "But aren't you going to say the words?" It was one of those times when only one book was being referred to, and no other could replace it. He wanted some scriptural references on which he could face the new experience of entering a new world of continued life. I quoted Isaiah 43:1-4:

> But now thus says the Lord, he who created you, O Jacob, he who formed you, O Israel: "Fear not, for I have redeemed you; I have called you by name, you are mine. When you pass through the waters I will be with you; and through the rivers, they shall not overwhelm you; . . . For I am the Lord your God, the Holy One of Israel, your Savior."

So Isaiah's experience with God was renewed in my father-in-law as he appropriated this faith. The Bible is a book where a person can hear God speak and can respond in faith and love.

In biblical literature God is portrayed as seeking right relationships between himself and persons, between man and man. This theme of right relationship is often referred to as "covenant." The concept of God's covenant, right relationships, assumes different patterns or configurations during the centuries with kaleidoscopic grandeur, mystery, and relevance to the day in which it is renewed and rephrased.

As one reads the Bible with a mind open to right relationships with God and with his fellow man his life becomes different, he's a new person, a new being. Such a person learns to set his thoughts (his mind) against the touchstone of the "Mind which was in Jesus Christ, our Lord" in order that his decisions may be made in the light and love of the Christ-like God.

Thus the question "What is the Bible?" becomes entirely different from a historical or literary or statistical study of sixty-six books. The Bible is the place where man encounters the living Word! As he responds affirmatively to that encounter he finds his authentic, true self. Man becomes alive, he becomes a new being. Such a man has learned how to use his Bible.

HOW WAS THE BIBLE WRITTEN?

The attitudes which we hold about how the Bible was written may be an asset or a barrier to hearing the Word. A wrong attitude may put the Word behind iron bars. What we need and want is the biblical view of how the Bible was written, for that will tell us how we are to handle the Word.

There are basically two differing views as to how the Bible was written. The nonbiblical view assumes that man had little or nothing to do with the writing of our Scriptures. It was written totally by divine intervention in human affairs. This view assumes that God used his writers as though they were merely instruments or robots emptied of their intelligence. Some think that our Gospels (including Luke) were written by some kind of automatic writing. Luke, some say, sat down at a desk, took pen in hand with paper before him, and momentarily lost his consciousness (at least control of his hand) while the Holy Spirit moved his hands and pen across the page. Luke thus wrote automatically, without any foreknowledge of his own of the events about which he was writing. Of course, since God was doing the writing the words that were finally printed were inerrant and infallible. This view of automatic writing denies the human element, emphasizing God's sole part in the writing of the Gospel. Hal Lindsey represents this view. He writes that when John wrote Revelation he became uniquely dominated by the Holy Spirit. He became infallible, writing the very words God gave him.[1]

The biblical view refutes this nonbiblical position of automatic writing. The record is plain as to how Luke wrote. Luke specifically refutes the automatic writing theory by stating that he used various sources available to him. A careful study of Luke 1:1-4 shows that Luke compiled his gospel. Luke had traveled thousands of miles with the apostle Paul as his personal physician. Luke had listened to ministers (disciples), to eyewitnesses (apostles such as Peter and Thomas and such persons as Mark, James, the brother of Jesus who was head of the church in Jerusalem, and the brothers James and John who were cousins of Jesus). Luke wrote with restrained excitement to Theophilus. Luke states in his preface (1:1-4) that he read all written accounts he could get hold of and talked with all who had known or heard Jesus. "Having followed all things closely for some time past" he then sat down at his desk, with pen in hand, and carefully compiled his record using the Gospel of Mark as the basic outline for his compilation and carefully writing in material from his notes.

HOW LUKE WROTE HIS GOSPEL

Luke therefore tells us that his records were human records. His sources were not infallible, so his own record is not to be taken as infallible. Luke wrote his Gospel in A.D. 85—fifty-five years after the death of Jesus—so that many details were lost or unclear to the memories of those who had been in their thirties during Jesus' ministry. We note how such memories were deficient in the story of the women at the tomb on Easter morning. Luke 24:4 states that "two men stood by them in dazzling apparel"; Mark 16:5 states that there was a (not two) "young man sitting on the right side, dressed in a white robe"; while Matthew 28:2 states "an angel of the Lord descended from heaven and came and rolled back the stone, and sat upon it." It is obvious that the sources used by Matthew and Mark differed from those used by Luke. These details are not the important thing anyway; the important thing was that Christ was risen! Whether there was an angel, a young man, or two men at the tomb is insignificant to the fact of the Risen Lord. But the point must be made: the sources used by the gospel writers are not infallible; indeed they are fallible because fallible persons told the stories of these great events in the latter years of their lives when memories were all but accurate. We would err in trying to make these three passages say the same thing—make one man equal to one angel and they in turn equal to two men. God doesn't want us to be irrational in order to be religious! The communists are wrong: Christians can be intelligent as well as religious.

Understanding how Luke used sources known to him, but sometimes different from those used by Mark and Matthew, helps us deal with inconsistencies or contradictions in the text.

HOW FIRST AND SECOND CHRONICLES WERE WRITTEN

Let us look for a few minutes at the Old Testament too. The Bible suggests in a number of places, by inference, how it was written. The book of Chronicles clearly observes that it was a compilation from other history books; it was not composed by God or any one person. I have no doubt that God did put the thought of recording the past into the minds of the writers, who then read widely and compiled the sacred events which illustrate God's mighty acts in their life and history.

The chronicler (writer of first and second Chronicles) states clearly the documents which he used in compiling his history of the times of the Kings. For example, note the scrolls he used in compiling the history of Kings David and Solomon. First Chronicles 29:29 states that he used as his major sources for David the chronicles of Samuel the seer, the chronicles of Nathan the prophet, and the chronicles of Gad the seer. There was no composing or automatic writing here. If there were errors, they stemmed from his sources—which certainly made no claim to inerrancy or infallibility. The record is plain that the writer based his information on the best sources he knew and that he included material which he thought was sufficient and adequate, leaving many other historical points of interest out of his account.

We also know the sources used in writing about the times of King Solomon (II Chronicles 9:29): "the history of Nathan the prophet, and in the prophecy of Ahijah the Shilonite, and in the visions of Iddo the seer." The point of these references is to help Christians understand the biblical position concerning how the Bible was written. This biblical position readily disclaims infallibility and inerrancy, showing us how dependent the writers were on various historians from whose books they took various portions to complete their books—which is now called the Scriptures.

Today, when a college student writes a term paper he must footnote his sources. The writer of Chronicles did this for us, except he named the primary sources in the body of the text rather than in a footnote at the bottom of the page or at the end of the chapter. As we have seen how the writer of Chronicles used various historical documents in his writing of I and II Chronicles, so scholars have found that the first five books of the Old Testament were written in a similar fashion using several documents or traditions for compiling these books. Let us look at Genesis to see how this great book was compiled, as was Chronicles, from several sources. In doing so we free ourselves to face the fact of several varying accounts of the same incident. If we keep our minds closed to the fact of compilation of sources, our unbiblical attitudes will make us abuse the Scriptures in ways that were never intended by the writers or by the councils who canonized the Scriptures.

HOW THE PENTATEUCH WAS WRITTEN

Scholars have identified at least four major sources used in the Pentateuch, the first five books of the Old Testament. Three of these are found in great detail in Genesis. The one not found in Genesis is in Deuteronomy. We can identify the three sources as the J-traditions, E-traditions, and the priestly code.

The J-traditions represent the southern records kept in Jerusalem; the E-traditions were those records kept by priests in the northern kingdom (Israel) after the monarchy under Solomon was split into two parts by civil war. The priestly code represents a late editing of the combined works of J and E, about 430 B.C.

To help understand the position let us recall the centennial celebration of the Battle of Atlanta in 1964. I recall reading about a proposed drama which would commemorate the battle between the Confederates and the Union. To be accurate, I am told, historians from both North and South were solicited for their insights and understandings of this battle. But the northern and southern views did not always agree! Even chaplains' records from both North and South did not always report events in the same way. Both views were finally incorporated in the drama, realizing that the ultimate truth lay somewhere in between their accounts. Both accounts admitted there was a battle of Atlanta!

In the same way, after the monarchy under the leadership of Kings David and Solomon was divided into two kingdoms, records were kept of the two separate kingdoms, and also two different records of how the monarchy was divided and why. Each nation (Israel, the northern kingdom; and Judah, the southern kingdom) had its own king, its royal historians, and its own temples and sacred and royal scribes. Each nation kept its own records and wrote them from their own perspective. Priests, sincere ones too, differed as to details of events.

The house of Joseph (the northern kingdom, which named their nation after one of Joseph's sons, Ephraim) did not always agree with the portrayal of events by the house of Judah. A part of the ancient rivalry was probably due to two things: first, Joseph's son Ephraim was the offspring of an Egyptian woman, Asenath, whose father was a priest at On (Memphis), Egypt; second, the house of Joseph used the name *Elohim* for God, and the house of Judah used the name *Jahweh*. Both divine names were well known, yet were used for the most part according to whether or not one was a northerner or a southerner. This is the reason the temple and royal historical records are referred to as J-traditions (the *J*udean records using *J*ahweh for the divine name) and the E-traditions (the *E*phraim records using *E*lohim for the divine name).

The J-traditions were written toward the close of King Solomon's reign, about 930 B.C., and include a sharp criticism of his reign, especially Genesis 2-11.[2] The E-traditions were written about 725 B.C., shortly before the collapse of the northern kingdom in 721 B.C. Each of them related how God (Elohim/Jahweh) had redeemed them from the hands of the Egyptian pharaoh, had led them to the land promised to their forefather Abraham, and had given them the land of Canaan. The two historical accounts tell of the fulfillment of God's threefold promises to Abraham (Genesis 12, 15)—the land of Canaan for their homeland, the assurance that Abraham's descendants would be great in number, and that God would bless all mankind through his seed (interpreted by Christians to refer to the coming of the Messiah in the person of Jesus of

Nazareth). God gave Abraham assurance of an everlasting covenant to him and his descendants.

WHY INCONSISTENCIES EXIST

An illustration of how we are helped in reading the Bible by knowing that several different sources were used by different writers about the same event is found in the account of King David taking a census of his people. David felt the need to know how many soldiers he could muster for war, so he took a census of all the males of his monarchy. Two of our biblical books give different reasons for his having taken the census, and they cannot both be right. Second Samuel 24:1-2, which approved the Davidic dynasty which Samuel established in the name of God, states that the Lord incited David to number Israel and Judah. But I Chronicles 21:1, written in a period when the Davidic dynasty was no longer existent and was now frowned upon, states that the devil told David to take the census of Israel and Judah. Well, you can hardly say that he who urged David was both God and the devil! God is not the devil, nor is the devil God.

The point I am making is that it helps to be aware that many events are told twice or even three times—and told from two or three different perspectives. Details vary, inconsistencies do exist. But it helps to know why they exist. Not knowing about the use of several sources has caused people to abuse their Scriptures in strange ways—making up reasons or rationalizations to cover up the obvious discrepancies, contradictions, and inconsistencies in the text. Our text is a human text, written by human hands, from human sources (traditions and historical documents) about Israel's relationships with God, whom they experienced as their creator, judge, redeemer, and savior.

These facts help us deal with the matter of the inspiration and authority of the Scriptures.

We have noted elsewhere how Genesis 1 corrects Genesis 2 in the accounts of creation. The order of God's creative acts in chapter 1 are reversed in chapter 2. The theology of chapter 1 (the priestly tradition, written in the fifth century B.C.) is far advanced over the second chapter (the J-traditions written in 930 B.C.). God's creative act described in chapter 2 is quite anthropomorphic—God collects the dust of the earth into the form of a man and breathes life and spirit into the dust; in chapter 1 God makes man simply by saying let there be a man, and it was so. God is Spirit and is portrayed as acting as supreme Spirit in his creation.

The two writers of Genesis 1 and 2 both loved God, and both wrote with deep sincerity. But the writer of chapter 1 is far more sophisticated and undoubtedly much closer to the truth of the way God created. Likewise the two writers of Chronicles and Samuel were equally sincere men. Both men knew God, as is obvious from reading their texts, for we still meet God through their pages. Yet, both wrote from a different psychological and national perspective, so their writings exhibit a variety of details which differ from each other. Yet their faith in God is the same.

The different writers were inspired men, yet they were fallible men too. These men, inspired by their encounter and faith in the living God, interpreted the events and their significance from their individual perspectives. They saw the "light" differently.

THE IMPORTANCE OF THE MEDIUM

If four men face the sunlight as it filters through a large prism or through stained glass windows, each sees the sunlight, yet each may see the colors differently. If one is standing so that he sees the red, another sees the blue, another sees green, another yellow—each sees the light of God shining through, yet each sees it differently because the medium through which the light shines has colored the light.

Our varied experiences, our varied psychological structures, our varied cultural and racial backgrounds may place us in a position where the light of God we see shining through is colored by the medium through which his light shines. The ultimate truth is not in the specific colors seen but in the light itself. Withdraw the prism and you see the light in its full glory. Paul said of Jesus: This day have I seen the light of God reflected in the face of Jesus Christ. At the other extreme, Samuel's hacking of King Agag to pieces before the Lord shows the light of God having difficulty getting through this human medium. We have learned through Jesus that God wants us to love and to forgive our enemies, not hack them to pieces with a sword. God's will is the same yesterday, today, and forever. It was so in Samuel's day. But Samuel misunderstood it; he was wrong; King Saul undoubtedly was right when he wanted to let the captured king live (1 Samuel 15).

Realizing how fallible men, truly inspired by their encounter with God, interpreted these experiences according to the way they saw the light, we realize that all scripture is not of equal quality nor value. We must learn to "sift" the record. When we read Paul's command to women to keep still in church we sift out that remark, don't we? When we consider the tremendous contributions women make to the church in our day, we realize that Paul was reflecting the customs of his day rather than the light of God as seen in Jesus Christ. Paul's command that women not cut their hair is certainly not an imperative in my home. We learn to sift out what is insignificant, don't we? I'm calling on all of us to admit that we do this and to admit the implications which are there, namely: all scripture is not of equal value. In fact, all scripture should be tested by the life-style and teachings of Jesus. Jesus Christ is our authority.

Emil Brunner once remarked if you would hear the voice of

the great Caruso (whose voice was recorded on old platters in
"The Masters Voice Series") you must learn to distinguish
between the scratches of the needle on the old records and the
voice of the master, Caruso. So it is with the Bible. The
"scratches" must be recognized as incidental and not of equal
value with the real message. Paul's references to women,
which we have noted above, are such scratches on the record.
Learn to differentiate and evaluate those kinds of statements
from Paul's doctrines on justification by faith. Develop a discriminating mind as you study—or else you will find that you
are abusing rather than using the Bible.

Martin Luther advised that we should distinguish clearly
between the straw on which the baby Jesus slept and the
baby. Again, to distinguish between the water the baby is
being bathed in and the baby. Don't throw the baby out with
the bath water. Be discriminating. I had a professor tell me
one time, as we were reading Hebrew together, to develop a
sense of smell. This sounds crude at first, yet he made his
point to me.

John Wesley held a similar view of discrimination concerning what is of highest value and what may be of little or no
spiritual value in the Scriptures. Wesley stated that psalm 109
is unworthy to be prayed by the lips of a Christian. The writer
of this psalm was complaining to God because wicked persons
who made false claims against him went free. So he prayed
that God would:

> Appoint a wicked man against him;
>   let an accuser bring him to trial
> When he is tried, let him come forth guilty;
>   let his prayer be counted as sin!
> May his days be few;
>   may another seize his goods!
> May his children be fatherless,
>   and his wife a widow!
> May his children wander about and beg.

Wesley stated in one of his orders of worship that this psalm should not be used in worship. I suspect that Wesley was right, even though it is in our Bible. You see, the authority of the Scriptures is not whether a passage is in the Bible, but whether it measures up to the spirit of Jesus Christ. Would Jesus have prayed that way? As a matter of fact, he didn't. Not at Gethsemane, not on Calvary. He had learned to forgive his enemies even when under great unwarranted pain. Luther used a great phrase: *Was Christum treibet*—does the passage move you toward Christ?

HOW WERE THE BOOKS OF THE BIBLE CHOSEN?

Sometimes it helps us in our attitudes about how to use the Bible if we understand how the Bible came into being. Let us look at this matter.

The Hebrew Bible has three divisions: (1) the Law—the first five books of the Bible, generally known as the Pentateuch; (2) the Prophets; and (3) the Writings—a total of twenty-four books. The English Old Testament followed the topical arrangement of the Greek and Latin Bibles, but it contained a total of thirty-six books. Let us use the Hebrew division for this discussion.

The first book to be accepted as scripture was Deuteronomy. It was found in Solomon's Temple in 621 B.C. and was proclaimed to be the Word of God by a woman named Huldah. Earlier writings had existed, such as the histories of the Ephraim-traditions and the Judean-traditions—which incidentally were collated into one scroll about 650 B.C. But these writings, as those of Amos, Hosea, and Isaiah, were not regarded as scripture at this time.

When Ezra read the law in Jerusalem at the place called Watergate, ca. 400 B.C., he apparently read portions of the

Pentateuch (Genesis, Exodus, Leviticus, Numbers, and Deuteronomy), which is a great and masterful work compiled by a priest who lived in exile in Babylonia. He had taken the combined histories of the north and south (J- and E-traditions) and put them in a framework of his own devising. It was this great work which was read by Ezra in Jerusalem; 400 B.C. marks the date of the acceptance by Judaism of the Pentateuch as the inspired Word of God. Note that Deuteronomy had been accepted in 621 B.C., and now to it is added the other four books making the Pentateuch. The hearing of this Law and its acceptance by the people marked the "canonization" of the Torah. Judaism then became a people of the book. Jews, seeking to know God's will, would search through their Torah in order to discover it. This proved to be a very limited Bible for Samaritans, who accepted only the Pentateuch in Jesus' day, and also to the priests who held office in Herod's Temple in Jerusalem in Jesus' day. John the Baptist, for example, being the son of a priest (Zechariah) would have held only to the Torah as scripture. He did not accept the Prophets as scripture.

The second group of Hebrew writings to be canonized (accepted as a standard for faith and practice) was the Prophets. This group of writings consisted of the four historical books, "The Former Prophets"—Joshua, Judges, Samuel, and Kings—the four scrolls of "The Latter Prophets"—Isaiah, Jeremiah, Ezekiel, and the twelve "Minor Prophets" (such as Amos, Hosea, Micah, and others). This group of writings called the Prophets was accepted as scripture about 200 B.C.

The third group was called "the Holy Writings" and included ten separate works: poetry (Psalms, Proverbs, Job); the five scrolls (Songs of Solomon, Ruth, Lamentations, Ecclesiastes, Esther); prophecy (Daniel); and history (our Ezra, Nehemiah, Chronicles). These Holy Writings were added to the Torah and Prophets by the Jewish Council at Jamnia, in A.D. 90—less than five years after the writing of the

Gospels of Luke and Matthew and five years before the writing of the books of Revelation and the Gospel of John. Jesus' Bible did not include the Writings.

When the Holy Writings were added to the canon, the Christians simply adopted the Jewish decision, and the books became their sacred scriptures too. To be sure, many books were not admitted though some rabbis argued for them.

The New Testament books were chosen over a long period of time, too. The earlier collection included Paul's nine letters to particular churches (Philemon being the exception, although it was addressed to "the church [that meets] in your house"). Many scholars think that the one-time runaway slave Onesimus, whose master was Philemon, became the Bishop of Asia Minor. Bishop Onesimus collected Paul's letters and wrote a covering letter which we know as Ephesians (a letter addressed to all Christians everywhere). This was the first step in the development of our New Testament Scriptures. Though Paul's letters were venerated, they were not referred to as scripture until about A.D. 150.

The second step was the collection of the four gospels: Matthew, Mark, Luke, and John. These were accepted as scripture toward the end of the second century A.D., except by the Syrian Church. Tatian, of the Syrian Church, worked out a chronology of sayings and events using the content of the four gospels. This work was called the *Diatessaron*. The Syrians believed they had no need of the four gospels since they adopted this harmonizing of the gospels by Tatian.

The third step in obtaining the canonized scripture of the New Testament was the long process of choosing the rest of the documents. Various writings were drawn together around the apostle Paul or the Gospels. Some were retained, but others were dropped as early churchmen began to fix the writings that were considered authoritative (*i.e.*, canonical). However, the canon was not fixed until the last half of the fourth century A.D.

Meanwhile, several other gospels were written: the Gospel of Thomas, the Gospel of Peter, the Gospel of Mary, the Gospel of the Infancy, and others. As one reads them we readily agree they detract from rather than add to the knowledge of our Lord Jesus. Two examples will illustrate this: The Gospel of the Infancy, chapter 19, tells of a boy who was possessed by Satan. He was inclined to bite all that were present, and if none were present he would bite himself. One day James and Joses had taken the infant, the Lord Jesus, to play with other children. And the possessed boy, named Judas, came and sat down at the right hand of Jesus. Satan began to act upon Judas, so he started to bite the infant Jesus. But he was unable to do so, so he struck Jesus on the right side, so that the baby Jesus cried out. And in the same moment Satan went out of the boy and ran away like a mad dog. This same boy who struck Jesus and out of whom Satan went in the form of a dog, was Judas Iscariot, who betrayed him to the Jews. And the same side on which Judas had struck the baby was the side the Jews pierced with a spear. I don't find this story very edifying, do you?

The second story, chapter 16, tells of how Joseph, who was really a bad carpenter, usually took Jesus with him. For when Joseph had anything in his work that needed to be made longer or shorter or wider or narrower, the Lord Jesus would stretch his hand towards it, and presently it became as Joseph desired it. This addition to the days of Jesus' adolescence doesn't add anything helpful. It only complicates and makes impossible the doctrine that Jesus was truly human as well as truly divine.

The early church was forced to choose those books which reflected significance for faith. They turned thumbs down on such gospels as I have just noted. They also were forced to decide that some letters and gospels must be listed as canonical in order to meet some heresies that were developing in the second century. For example, the heretic Marcion, a wealthy

Christian shipowner from Sinope, went to Rome about A.D. 140. He taught that matter and spirit were evil and good respectively. Matter—the physical world including our bodies—was evil and therefore could not have been created by a good God. Spirit, being good, was created by the good God, the God of the New Testament. So Marcion, a Gnostic, abandoned the Old Testament, saying that the Creator God of the Old Testament was evil, ignorant, and hostile to the good God of the New Testament. This, of course, called for action.

Marcion accepted only one of the Gospels, that by Luke, which he "weeded" out in order to make it fit his beliefs. Marcion also accepted Paul and his writings. Paul's attacks on the Law were thought by Marcion to be attacks on the Old Testament. So the early church was obligated to decide which gospels and which letters were to be considered authoritative for the New Testament. They acted in response to the heresies of Marcion by declaring that all four gospels Matthew, Mark, Luke, and John were valid and that Paul's writings were valid. The Muratorian Canon, a list of New Testament books drawn up in Rome in A.D. 200, included the above four gospels, Paul's letters, Acts, the Pastoral Epistles (Timothy, Titus, Philemon), Jude, 1 and 2 John, and Revelation. But it omitted 1 Peter, James, 2 Peter, 3 John, and Hebrews.

THE CANON IS FIXED

The churchmen debated for over three hundred years about the book of Revelation, some saying it was unfit to be read (Marcion and the Alogi and Caius of Rome and Bishop Cyril of Jerusalem in A.D. 386), some saying it should be read only if it were allegorized (Origen), some saying it wouldn't hurt anybody if it were read (Eusebius), some saying it should be included in the list of New Testament Books (Tertullian, Irenaeus, and Cyprian). Revelation was not included in the Scriptures approved by the Synod of Laodicea in A.D. 360.

It was only ten years later that Athanasius of Alexandria (Egypt) in his thirty-ninth Festal Letter, written in A.D. 367, listed the twenty-seven books of our present New Testament canon. Early church fathers, such as Justin Martyr, Origen, Irenaeus, Tertullian, and Clement all had differing lists of books. We have accepted the list of twenty-seven books proclaimed as canonical by Athanasius of Alexandria, Bishop of the Greek Orthodox Church. The Syrian and Ethiopic Church still lists a different number of books than we do. The list of twenty-seven books for our New Testament were approved by the Provincial Council at Hippo, Africa, in A.D. 383, and at Carthage in 392. The list was not approved by an ecumenical council. Other Christians adopted the list which the friendly and persuasive Bishop Athanasius had written as his list of sacred books for the New Testament.

The canon was closed because the churchmen felt that this was the way to stop heretical writings (such as Marcion's writings, and other gospels such as the Infancy) from becoming canonized too. So the church adopted the policy that any book or letter written after the times of the apostles would not be canonical. The canon was closed! The latest letter to be accepted was written about A.D. 125. Tertullian believed that the Holy Spirit still moved among people and could urge them to write letters which would be appropriate as New Testament material. Tertullian said rather vitriolically: The Holy Spirit has been chased into a book [the New Testament].

The point being emphasized was that in the days when the apostles lived and wrote, or when persons wrote down their memories of what the apostles had said (such as Luke and as Mark did for Peter), the Holy Spirit guided the writing of the sacred books. But after the apostolic days the Holy Spirit no longer guided men to write; rather the Spirit enabled them to interpret (exegete) and make commentaries on the words which had been written. I might comment that these were manmade decisions as to what God could or could not do or did or did not do! Does a church body decide what God can do? Perhaps it is up to each person to decide whether God has stopped inspiring persons to write of the Risen Lord, as when Paul who lived after the days when Jesus lived in the flesh, wrote his letters. What do you think?

It is helpful to know that the choosing of the sacred books was not a matter of having certain unique books handed down from heaven on a golden platter. The process of choosing was difficult and arduous work. Debate raged many times. And for some the canon is still not closed. Martin Luther said the letter of James was a work of straw and wasn't worth being read. John Calvin said that the Book of Revelation was unworthy of a Christian's time and should not be read.

Does it really matter if a book was or is accepted as scripture? Dr. Martin Rist in his introduction to the book of Revelation states the case cogently:[3]

> From the middle of the second century, if not earlier, it was a mysterious and disputed book. On the other hand, there can be little question that its first readers, those persecuted Christians to whom it was originally addressed, experienced little difficulty in understanding and appreciating its message; for not only were they, like its author, steeped in apocalyptic thought and imagery, but the book was directed toward their own precarious situation. But when the time and situation for which it was written had passed, its acceptance as scripture created difficulties which persist to the present day. For by being canonized Revelation became a divinely inspired and therefore authoritative series of predictions of what was to occur at some time in the future, with the interpreter's, not the author's time tending to be the point of departure. Likewise, as scripture its depiction of God and Christ, of Satan and Antichrist, of angels and demons and other supernatural powers commanded acceptance. In the same manner its portrayal of the universe in which we live, of heaven and hell, of the present age and the age to come, and of the millennium, with its philosophy of history, claimed the attention of believers. These distinctive ideas of the writer created difficulties which would scarcely have arisen had Revelation remained outside of the canon; for then it would have been understood and interpreted with reference to the histor-

ical situation which produced it and the purpose the author had in its composition. In other words, it would have been studied as objectively as uncanonical, nonscriptural apocalypses like I Enoch, II Baruch, the Apocalypse of Peter, or the Ascension of Isaiah are studied. Even though II Esdras is in the Old Testament Apocrypha, its quasi-canonical status has made possible its being studied and interpreted quite objectively. But unfortunately, the canonical position of both Revelation and Daniel has been largely responsible for the artificial, subjective, and arbitrary manner in which they have been treated, not only by Christians in general but also by the majority of scholars down through the centuries.

This quotation from the popular *Interpreter's Bible* illustrates a modern scholar's attitude similar to Calvin's attitude toward the canon: men, not God, made the decision as to the content of the canon.

Understanding of the debates of churchmen and church councils (provincial and ecumenical) should help us be more tolerant of those with whom we have disagreement. It also acts as a red flag of caution lest we too easily or too quickly make decisions which may cause us to abuse the Bible, devaluing or even distorting the best and most valuable sections of the Scriptures.

When a person, in reading scripture, is aware that he is experiencing encounter with the mighty and loving God, has checked his experience with other scriptures (for a total view of the gospel), has seen the passage in the light of tradition and the strictures of reason—he should rejoice. Immanuel! God has been with him. This is the goal of Bible study—to know the loving God and do his will.

SOME ABUSES OF SCRIPTURE

Now let us consider some misuses or abuses of scripture. I suggest four: allegory, typology, analogy, and inadequate expectations from reading the Bible.

Allegorizing the Scripture

The early church fathers, especially in the second and third centuries A.D., abused the scriptures by use of allegory. Illustrations will help us to understand the method of allegory and its abuse of scripture.

Dr. John Bright illustrates the "exotic jungle" of allegorizing: while Israel fought Amalek, Moses, sitting with outstretched arms, became weary, so his arms were supported by his brother Aaron and a friend Hur (Exodus 17:8-16). The outstretched arms formed the sign of the cross. Tertullian, Justin, and the others said it was by this sign of the cross that Amalek was overcome by Jesus (Joshua) through Moses. The harlot Rahab let down a scarlet cord from her house in Jericho. By this scarlet cord, which symbolized the redemption of sinners through the blood of Jesus, the spies were saved (Joshua 2:6). Furthermore, Irenaeus said that the spies were doubtless the three persons of the Trinity and Rahab was the church, whose members are harlots and other sinners.[4]

The great saint Augustine of the latter part of the fourth century A.D. also used allegory. He allegorized the parable of the Good Samaritan in this fashion:

A certain man (meaning Adam) went down from Jerusalem (the city of peace from which Adam fell) to Jericho (our human mortality toward which Adam goes) and fell among thieves (the devil and his angels who stripped him of his immortality and beat him into sinfulness, leaving him stripped of close fellowship with God). Soon some Levites and priests (the priesthood of the Old Testament) came by, but he (Adam) received no help from them. Finally a Samaritan (Jesus) comes and binds up his wounds (restraints to sin are placed upon him), and oil (the comfort of hope) and wine (new spirit) is given the man (Adam). He (Adam) is placed on a beast (humanity is carried by faith in the Incarnation) and is taken to the inn (the church). . . .

This is indeed an exotic jungle of interpretation. To allegorize scripture is to lose the reader in the game of "this means that" so that the reader completely forgets that God was speaking directly to him through the parable of the Good Samaritan. The meaning of the parable for our daily choices of moral and spiritual concern is lost—and thus allegory abuses the Scriptures. It is my judgment that we should not use allegory at all—it misleads, distorts, and stultifies the Word. Allegory imprisons the Word so that the Holy Spirit cannot move freely in the mind of the reader.

The great reformers, Luther and Calvin, rejected allegorizing of both Old and New Testaments. They argued that it is the duty of the interpreter of the Bible to offer the plain sense of the text, the meaning intended by its author. Luther was pretty harsh with Origen's allegorical method of interpreting scripture. Luther said allegory was "not worth so much dirt"; he considered allegory as "the scum of scripture," as a "harlot" to seduce us, a "monkeygame."

Use of Typology

Both Calvin and Luther, escaping the perils and abuses of allegory, tripped up in their interpretation of scripture via typology. These reformers sought impressive parallels between Old Testament events and those of the New Testament. Such parallels were seen as the following: Adam's temptations were renewed in Jesus' temptations; the beasts of the Garden of Eden were found in the wilderness where Jesus was being tempted (Mark 1:13); the angels of the Garden of Eden ministered unto Jesus; David the King prefigured Christ the King; Joseph prefigured the saving power of Christ, etc. I well recall using this typological approach in my first year of biblical study in postgraduate study. I now consider it an inferior way of interpreting scripture. Indeed it is an abuse of scripture.

Typology demands a certain cleverness to be able to read New Testament events back into the original types in the Old

Testament. Of course there are correspondences between many Old Testament events and those of the New Testament, but this is quite different from a system of typology which we have just noted.

Use of Analogy

Closely related to the allegorical method of interpreting scripture is that of analogy. It, too, is a questionable way of interpreting scripture. Yet great Christian persons have used it as their principle of interpreting the Word. One of these great Christian leaders is the late Karl Barth. Barth's use of analogy differs from Augustine's method of allegory. Barth (in his *Dogmatic IV*, 2, 21 ff) suggests that Luke in his parable of the prodigal son intended more than the obvious. Luke, says Barth, intended that the younger son should represent the Gentile world, the older son the Jews. This in turn suggests a Christological interpretation that was not originally intended, namely: the younger son is identified with Jesus. The descent of the son into the far country reminds us (by analogy) of the descent of the Son of God from the heavenly Father. Jesus, identifying himself with sinners (fallen man), rises out of humiliation into glory, finding a seat at the right hand of the Father. The possibility of a sinner's returning to his father is dependent upon the reality of Christ's return to the Father.

So analogizes Karl Barth. This kind of interpretation, while quite clever and ingenius, only confuses. It also blocks the Holy Spirit from speaking his message which the parable of the prodigal son was intended to teach. I personally think this is an abuse of scripture; it keeps us from properly using scripture.

Inadequate Expectations from Bible Reading

One's conception of revelation may lead him astray in reading the Bible too. The rationalist seeks for eternal truths and/or principles which he can separate from the context of the passage. The orthodox theologian studies the Bible hoping to find good ore from which he can smelt propositional statements about God, man, sin, salvation. The psychologist tries to penetrate the psyche of Jesus to understand the motives that ruled his actions, the hopes that drew him to the cross. Today scholars are finding a new and fresh emphasis: scripture reveals more than eternal truths and principles, more than doctrines, more than the inner psyche of Jesus; scripture reveals God. The whole purpose of revelation is to experience the presence of God. Immanuel! God is with us! This suggests a basic attitude if we would use our Bible aright: we must be willing to be sensitive to the leading of the Holy Spirit. We must be willing to look at the historical events of Old and New Testament times with the "eyes of faith"—to see men of faith and especially Jesus Christ through the eyes of those who knew him, through the eyes of the faith of the early church whose members wrote our New Testament documents.

EISEGESIS OR EXEGESIS?

Another abuse of scripture is to substitute eisegesis for exegesis. Exegesis is a critical (scholarly) explanation or analysis of a passage. The exegete asks "What does this particular passage of scripture say—both to persons at the time it was written and to us now."

Eisegesis differs from exegesis in that it brings to a passage of scripture ideas which were never intended in the original. When these ideas are superimposed on the passage, they distort and diminish the truths of that text.

Consider Matthew 25:31-46. Matthew 25 relates three parables dealing with preparedness (25:1-13), the use of capabilities (25:14-30), the importance of concern and love for others as a condition for eternal life (25:31-36).

Matthew 25:31-46 is a challenging parable told by Jesus to make one point very clear: moral choices which a person and nation make in response to persons in need is a major factor in God's evaluation of a person's or nation's life. The question to be asked is whether or not you were concerned enough to feed the hungry, clothe the naked, give a drink to the thirsty, welcome the strangers, visit those in prison. Jesus was challenging his hearers to a faith in God which embraces God's concerns, which include the hungry, the naked, the imprisoned, the unemployed, the alienated. Jesus called for an involvement in the needs of all suffering humanity.

A contemporary writer illustrates how eisegesis distorts and diminishes the truth of this passage. This writer brings his own ideas about who "these my brethren" are and superimposes this meaning on the passage. "These my brethren," he writes, refer to the 144,000 Jewish evangelists who are converted at the Rapture (seven years before the second coming of Jesus). These Jews, brothers of the Jewish Jesus, will be concerned about the lost (unconverted) Jews of Israel. These 144,000 Jewish evangelists will preach to their Jewish countrymen during the seven-year Tribulation. These Jewish evangelists will be like 144,000 Billy Grahams turned loose all at one time. But, he says, they will be persecuted terribly. They will be hungry, naked, imprisoned, sick. How persons treat these Jewish evangelists, "my brethren," will reflect whether he or she is a Christian, and hence whether they will be saved or not. So, Christians beware during the seven-year Tribulation which follows the Rapture.[5]

To interpret the parable of Matthew 25:31-46 as a passage speaking about 144,000 Jews to be converted sometime in the future after the Rapture and how they should be treated during the seven-year Tribulation is to distort and destroy the message of Jesus' parable which focused on the need for all persons of all nations to be involved in liberating the sick, the oppressed, the alienated, all persons on the face of the earth.

Eisegesis we don't need. Eisegesis is a red herring—it draws us away from the real issue. Sound exegesis we do need.

VALUE OF LITERARY AND HISTORICAL CRITICISM

Some Christians discount the use of literary and historical criticism of the Bible. Probably this negative attitude arises from misunderstanding of what such criticism seeks to do and the method by which these disciplines do their work.

Biblical scholars, who are at home in various languages (Hebrew, Aramaic, Greek, Latin, as well as German, French, and English), seek to understand the meaning of original words and phrases. They want to know when a writer of a biblical book or letter lived, to whom he wrote, and what he hoped his writing would achieve. Bible scholars in using higher criticism also want to know what insights archaeological discoveries can bring to the biblical text—new insights as to various cultures, religious artifacts, and theologies are expressed in their written religious literature.

The Bible scholar who has a wide background in languages, archaeology, Eastern religions as well as political and sociological history of Bible times is best able to offer reliable exegesis, interpretations, and commentary on the scriptures. The exegete needs his Bible and all the additional scholarly aids he or she can get. The person who uses these extra aids is engaged in higher criticism. So the phrase "higher criticism" is a good, helpful, and affirmative one.

An example may help: consider how higher criticism aids in the exegesis of Isaiah 14:1-20. It is a mocking dirge directed to the king of Babylon. This king and his armies had terrorized the nations for decades. The first stanza of the poem declares that the Lord has caused the oppressor to cease; "The Lord has broken the staff of the wicked ... that ruled the nations in anger with unrelenting persecution" (vss. 5, 6). The whole earth, even the trees of the forest, rejoices that this terror has been stopped short (vss. 4b-8).

The second stanza mockingly tells of the mighty king of

Babylon's reception after his death in Sheol. Shades, or ghosts, of kings defeated by the king of Babylon rise from their spectral thrones to look at him. Their ghostly eyes wandered up and down his spectral body, now devoid of royal garments of scarlet and his usual earthly jewels of royalty. The former kings previously defeated by the king of Babylon, greet him. Where now in the grave is the pomp and circumstance of his former pride and arrogance? "Is this the man who made the earth tremble, who shook kingdoms?" (vs. 16b.) Where now is the pomp and pride of Babylon? The great ruler is as weak now as are the other kingly shades in Sheol.

And what in the long run had the great Babylonian king achieved? Dr. G. G. D. Kilpatrick summarized the King's success in these words:

> He won the supremacy of his world; he had everything—unlimited treasure, absolute power, undisputed possession of human lives. But at what cost! On a bloodstained throne he sat, friendless, feared, forelorn, and when he died the world echoed with thanksgiving that he was gone, and all men celebrated his death with curses.[6]

The third stanza continues the taunt song against the king of Babylon. This time the prophet uses a literary device called "Mashal." This Mashal (vss. 12-21), a poem, makes a mocking comparison between the King of Babylon and a small star named Helel (in Hebrew), or Helal (Ugaritic).

Isaiah's readers would have known about "Helal, Son of Shahar." Archaeologists help us here: In ancient Ugaritic texts Canaanite religious literature speaks of Helal the Day Star or Lightgiver. This nature myth tells of the attempt of the morning star [Helal], son of Dawn, to scale the heights of heaven, surpassing all other stars only to be cast down to earth by the victorious sun.[7]

This ancient Canaanite story about Day Star's prideful attempts to reach the heights of heaven is used by Isaiah by way of poetic analogy to show the pride, arrogance, and fall of the mighty and arrogant King of Babylon.

> Isaiah 14:12: "How *you* [king of Babylon!] are fallen from
>   heaven,
>   O Day Star [Helel] son of Dawn [Shahar].
>   How you are cut down to the ground,
>   You who laid the nations low!"

> Isaiah 14:10*b*: "You [king of Babylon] too have become weak
>   as we!
>   Your pomp is brought down to Sheol."

The "you" of the second word in Isaiah 14:12 refers to "you" in verse 10*b* which is speaking of the king of Babylon; "you" in verse 12 refers to the Babylonian king who is now poetically called "O Day Star" (Helel in Hebrew and Helal in Canaanite language, or Lucifer in Greek and Latin).

The king of Babylon, only a mortal, thought to make himself as powerful as God in the historical events of earth. He wanted to act as though he, a mortal, were God: "I will make myself like the most High" (14:14*b*).

The prophet Isaiah declared in several chapters (including chapters 13 and 14) that the Lord, not man, is the Lord of history. The arrogant, hateful, merciless oppressor may have his day, but the future belongs to God; the future of the oppressor is ignominy, emptiness, and hatred. Now let us move from the above exegesis which is informed by archaeological discoveries to a modern example of eisegeses.

EISEGESIS ON THE BIRTH OF SATAN

We are told by some popular interpreters of the Bible that Isaiah 14 is a pivotal point in the history of our earth. The taunt song "O Day Star, Son of Dawn" refers, they say, to Lucifer. They say that the ancient myth of a presumptuous star rising so high that it was thrown back to its proper place by the sun is to be taken literally: that is, Lucifer sought God's throne and was thrown out of heaven on God's orders. In this view Isaiah 14 is not a taunt song against the king of Babylon, as the text clearly states, but is an account of the birth of Satan.[8] The Greek and Latin (Vulgate) translations (which were made many centuries later) of Isaiah 14 do use the name "Lucifer," which is the equivalent of "Day Star" or "Morning Star," but not Satan.

To turn the taunt song of Isaiah 14 into a theology of the fall of Satan from heaven is a distortion and abuse of scripture. It misleads the uncritical Bible reader.

Hal Lindsey also considers Ezekiel 28:11-15 a description of the fall of Satan. Yet this passage, as in Isaiah 14, is a taunt song. Ezekiel's taunt song is clearly addressed to the king of Tyre, a Phoenician city on the coast of the Mediterranean Sea. Ezekiel's taunt song is also a song of comparison or analogy, as was the case with Isaiah 14. The analogy shows how the fabulously rich and cruel king of Tyre was at one time a good and successful man; but his successes in lucrative trade led him to pride, arrogance, and violence. Let us note the historical background of the Phoenicians.

For a thousand years Phoenicia had been noted for its fabulous trading business by ships. Phoenician ships plied the seas from scores of harbors around the world. As such, the Phoenician kings became quite wealthy. With their wealth these rulers adorned themselves with the best of jewels found throughout the world (Ezekiel 28:13). So the prophet Ezekiel taunted both the prince and the king of Tyre as Isaiah had mocked the king of Babylon. Ezekiel also used analogy as he described the king as being like Adam in the beginning of his life: "You were in Eden, the garden of God;" "You were the signet of perfection;" "*with* an anointed guardian cherub I placed you [in Eden]" (vss. 12, 13, 14). The king was a man of wisdom and personal beauty, but pride in his lucrative mercantile business caused him to become arrogant and evil. Both shrewd and skilled in trade, the king acted with violence and mercilessness. So "the guardian cherub drove you out . . . your heart was proud." The moral of the analogy of the king of Tyre with Adam is the doom which comes to those, originally good and capable leaders, who become violent, oppressive, and merciless persons. The sinner reaps the reward of God's judgment: God sets his face and purposes against the evil person.

Contrast this exegesis with the eisegesis of Hal Lindsey which substitutes Lucifer for the king of Tyre. Lindsey adds his own ideas to the passage and claims this passage designates Lucifer as the "anointed cherub" who is the ruler and leader of the angelic beings. Moreover he states that Lucifer was the choir director in heaven! Lucifer [again note: Lucifer was substituted without any good reason for the king of Tyre!] was the greatest being God ever created of unequaled strength, wisdom, beauty, and authority. Compare this translation with the Revised Standard Version's translation.

Lindsey, pursuing his eisegesis states that the fallen angel, Lucifer, then sought to rule the world; indeed Satan (Lucifer) does rule the earth, and has ruled since the fall of Adam.[9]

I ask if the above interpretation by Lindsey is not an abuse of scripture? With the lack of knowledge of archaeological backgrounds, misleading and distorted interpretations are made. We need all the insights higher criticism (scholarship) can give us as we read the Bible in search of understanding of the will and purposes of God.

We might add two further implications of Lindsey's interpretation of Isaiah 14:12-15. First, Satan, the fallen leader of fallen angels, fell to earth. Here he rules, while Jesus Christ and God rule in heaven (as absentee Lords of earth). With Lucifer's fall, earth was polluted by him and had to be reconstructed from the chaos in which he had left it. So Genesis 1, 2 describe not the creation but the reconstruction of planet earth, on which planet God made man on the sixth day of creation.[10]

Secondly, man was created so that God could prove to the angels in heaven that he is a God of perfect love and to show the angelic beings who chose to stay with him that he had not been unjust nor unloving to Satan and his followers in his judgments which condemned Lucifer to eternal banishment. God's love would be demonstrated through a man at Golgotha.[11]

The old *arguementum ad absurdum* (argument of absurdity) helps us again. Surely God's motives in making persons was far superior to this motivation of defending his honor. God made man in his image that persons might choose to be like God in spirit, motive, disposition, spiritual beauty, and humility. God made persons that they might choose to become like Christ—Christ-like human beings.

SCIENCE AND THE BIBLE

Perhaps a word of caution should be spoken concerning the relation of scientific statements and the Bible. The Bible is not a textbook in science. It was not written by a geologist or a biologist or an astronomer or a physicist. The Bible is best thought of as a record of man's encounters with God and his mighty acts in their behalf. The Bible should not be expected to give answers to such questions as the age of the world or the process by which God made it. We may ask of the Bible, not how or when, but why and who. The how and when questions belong to the descriptive sciences, such as molecular biology (with its insights in the DNA molecule), chemistry (with its analysis of the structure of molecules), geology (which gives us the age of the earth), or nuclear physics (which describes atomic structures), or astronomy (which tells us of the creation and age of the universe). Faith answers the why and who questions. It postulates God as the Creator, Designer, Judge, Redeemer—the personal cause and purposer of all that exists. Through the Bible we learn that God is not only Creator but the kind of God who purposes, plans, cares, yearns, hopes, loves, hates, redeems, is thwarted, is personal, and yearns for fellowship with those made in his image! God is like Christ; Christ is like God.

Through the Bible we encounter God again and again in and through its pages. On the written page we read of how others encountered God. And soon we realize that we too are encountering this divine presence in our time. The greatest value in properly using the Bible is the fact that through the reading we come to know God and his will for our individual and corporate lives and can become participants with him in the work of making the kingdoms of this world become the kingdoms of our Christ.

There are times when various scriptures conflict with each other or seem inadequate. How do we know what to do? John Wesley developed four guidelines which he used for doctrinal statements. I find these same four guidelines helpful in interpreting difficult passages of scripture. First let me state that Wesley did not accept scripture alone. Albert Outler has said the *sola scriptura* did not mean "nothing but scripture." Wesley read scripture through the eyes of a biblical scholar with an awareness of church tradition. Wesley tested scriptural insights in the crucible of personal experience. And he sought to understand them within the strictures of reason.

Of all affirmations Wesley demanded that they be rooted in the Bible, be illumined by tradition, realized in experience, and confirmed by reason—all together, none apart from the others. This, says Dr. Outler, is why a Methodist has actually abandoned the Wesleyan tradition if and when he turns biblicist or traditionalist or existentialist or rationalist. Such a person has also repudiated Wesley's "Catholic Spirit" when he starts berating persons with other views or practices that do not contradict the Christian basics.

I suggest that helpful guidelines for the interpretation of the Bible include the four just referred to: what do other scripture passages say (that is, see one passage in the light of the whole gospel, not as an isolated part of it); how have the traditions of the church dealt with it; test its insights in the crucible of personal experience; understand the passage within the strictures of reason. These four guidelines can help us to use, not abuse, the Scriptures.

SUGGESTIONS FOR GROUP DISCUSSION

1. Discuss the author's statement that our attitudes may be an asset or a barrier to hearing God's word. How can attitudes imprison the Word? Free the Word?

2. Ask two students from the sixth grade to explain their understanding of what the Bible is. Their teacher might help them make their reports.

3. Do you have "biblical" problems with Paul's statement that women should keep silent in church? And that women should ask their husbands for correct instructions and understanding of the gospel? Would Wesley's four theological guidelines help: (a) What do other passages of scripture say? (b) What have church traditions said? (c) What, in your personal and church experience, would happen if this advice were followed? (d) What does your best reasoning suggest?

4. Can you accept Martin Luther (who considered the letters of James as "so much straw"), John Calvin (who considered Revelation unworthy for study), and John Wesley (who stated that Psalm 109 should not be used for the devotional life) as Christians? Did they have a right to make decisions about which books of the Bible are worthy or not worthy? What if a contemporary Christian made such a suggestion?

5. What do you think about "abuses of scripture"?

6. Does it really matter which biblical version, translation, or paraphrase you use for study? In what way do some of the current paraphrases of the Bible engage in eisegesis? Does this help explain or distort the message? Compare translations

of the Revised Standard Version, Our Living Bible, and the
New English Bible (for example: Ezekiel 28 and Isaiah 14).

NOTES

[1] Hal Lindsey, *There's a New World Coming* (Santa Ana, Cal.: Vision House
Publishers, 1973), p. 33. Note p. 23 where he contradicts himself.

[2] Cf. Horace R. Weaver, *The Everlasting Covenant* (Nashville: Graded
Press, 1965), pp. 82-87.

[3] Nolan B. Harmon, ed., *The Interpreter's Bible*, XII (Nashville: Abingdon
Press, 1957), 353.

[4] For other illustrations see the excellent work of John Bright, *The Authority
of the Old Testament* (Nashville: Abingdon Press, 1967), p. 81.

[5] Lindsey, *There's a New World Coming*, pp. 120, 264.

[6] *The Interpreter's Bible* 5, 263; note also Scott's exegesis, pp. 261-263.

[7] *Ibid.*, p. 262.

[8] Lindsey, *Satan Is Alive and Well on Planet Earth* (Grand Rapids, Mich.:
Zondervan, 1974), p. 33.

[9] Lindsey, *There's a New World Coming*, pp. 26, 91, 150, 152; *see also Satan
Is Alive and Well on Planet Earth*, p. 48.

[10] Lindsey, *Satan Is Alive and Well on Planet Earth*, pp. 38, 41.

[11] *Ibid.*, p. 40.

WHAT ABOUT THE RAPTURE, THE SECOND COMING, 666 . . .

(Finding Meaning in Apocalyptic Literature)

We have previously noted various ways persons abuse or use the Scriptures. Perhaps the books of Daniel and Revelation are the prime examples of our abuse of scripture. Popular books, written all too often by biblically uneducated writers, distort the purpose and the message of the authors. These popular writers superimpose their own unlearned ideas and eschatological time schedules on the biblical texts and refuse to recognize the relevance of the biblical message for the days of confusion and bewilderment for which time the books were written. This chapter seeks to help persons understand how to read, understand, and use apocalyptic literature, with special reference to the books of Daniel and Revelation.

The Bible may be thought of as a library of sixty-six books. It contains books on such subjects as law, history, devotional material, gospels, letters, and apocalypse. Apocalypse is quite different from any other literature found in the Bible. Apocalypse means hidden, hence it suggests mystery. So the search for hidden mystery is very popular in our day.

In apocalyptic writings of the Old Testament we find Daniel's description of four beasts rising from the sea, raised by the four winds of earth. We read about a lion with two eagles' wings, a bear with three ribs in its mouth, a leopard with four heads and four wings, and a ferocious beast with ten horns, three of which are rooted out by a new and smaller horn. Revelation speaks of two beasts rising out of the sea. The first has seven heads, is smitten yet revives, and has ten crowns. A second beast rises from the sea also, but serves the first. Then there is war in heaven between God and a dragon, but this is preceded by the "Rapture" [I Thessalonians 4:16-

17] and followed by the opening of seven seals, the blowing of seven trumpets, the opening of seven vials, the seven dooms, the coming of the heavenly Christ (the second coming), a millenium, and finally a new heaven and a new earth.

The question is: How can we find meaning in apocalyptic literature? How can we understand the references to beasts, horns, and trumpets, rapture, the second coming, the victory of Christ in his battle against the dragon? What do they mean? How should we interpret them?

I find it helpful in understanding apocalyptic literature and in appropriating its message to keep in mind some basic presuppositions: The first is the world view (cosmology) held by biblical man of 2,000-2,500 years ago; the second is the view we modern persons hold of our universe. Also, we need to keep in mind some theological affirmations taught by the prophets and especially by Jesus Christ. Let us begin our study by thinking about these two basic concerns: the varying world views and the theological affirmations which guide our thinking as we study scripture.

TWO VIEWS OF OUR WORLD

Modern man believes that our universe is probably finite, bounded, and elliptical in shape. Einstein suggested that our universe is possibly several billion light years in circumference. Our universe is composed of millions of solar systems. Our universe is quite different from that conceived in apocalyptic literature.

At one time the ancients believed in three, sometimes in seven, heavens. Paul once talked about being lifted up into the third heaven. Biblical man conceived of a flat, four-square earth—not a biosphere as our astronauts have seen it from the moon. Biblical man assumed our earth to be surrounded by water (the fearful sea, which was inhabited by great and fearful beasts). Under the earth was Hades (Sheol in Hebrew) where the dead lived a shadowy existence. Above the earth were three (or seven) heavens. The highest heaven contained the throne of God. On either side of God were twelve elders—the four and twenty elders who occasionally cast their golden crowns upon the glassy sea. Millions of beings served God, and other millions worshiped him.

In one of the heavens, biblical man thought the lights (sun, moon, planets, and stars) were hung out at night. The Babylonians, who loved astrology, believed that the planets themselves were deities who governed the lives of persons on earth. From this conception of planets being living gods has arisen the modern big business of predicting and selling horoscopes.

So, persons of two thousand years ago were taught that God was transcendent, far removed from the concerns of earth. It is time we confess and affirm that the shape of the universe (both heaven and earth) is not as it was believed to be by the apocalyptist. Most of us will admit that we cannot hold to that ancient cosmology. Our astronauts who have been in outer space know that this older view of our world is not true.

Titov, the first Russian spaceman to go around our earth in a spacecraft, declared: "I have searched the heavens but could find no angels, nor could I find the throne of God." Of course he didn't find the throne of God. The throne of God isn't up in the sky, nor is God "up there" somewhere in the sky.

Suppose you were standing at the north pole and you wanted to pray to God. You might look up toward the heavens to pray. Contrast your physical stance with a person standing

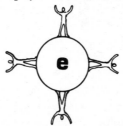

Figure 6

at the south pole who also wants to pray. He too looks toward heaven and stretches his arms toward the great white throne. Yet both men are pointing in opposite directions. If you were at the equator and your feet were firmly planted on the earth and you were standing erect, with hands raised toward the heavens and the throne of grace, well, which direction is heaven? This is a good example of the logical fallacy called *argumentum ad absurdum*. Our conclusion leads to absurdity. Our trouble is not our logic, but the primary premise of our argument.

What's wrong with this faith-claim of locating God in one place? Our answer lies in the teachings of the prophets, such as Isaiah, and in the teachings of Jesus Christ. God is Spirit. God is nonphysical. As Spirit God is not localized in any one place, as on a physical throne in one spot of the heavens. God is all around us, isn't he? Let us affirm the experience of Immanuel. God is *with* us! God is very real, very personal, and very near to each of us.

When a pastor visits an ill person, he has no need to cry out with a loud voice to arouse the deity far off in the sky to stop and listen to his cry. Rather, he presupposes the presence of God. He prays that the sick person may also affirm that underneath are the everlasting arms of God. God is very near—as close as life and breath.

I was once asked to consider using a picture of Jesus for the cover of *Adult Bible Studies*. This person wanted Jesus portrayed with long white hair, for Revelation 1:14 states that his hair is white as snow, white as wool. But consider the rest of that verse and the kind of painting that would attempt to portray Jesus Christ: "his eyes were like a flame of fire, his feet were like burnished bronze, refined as in a furnace, and his voice was like the sound of many waters; . . . from his mouth issued a sharp two-edged sword." Isn't this a metaphor, rather than actual portrayal? I think so. It represents the heavenly Christ as being of great wisdom, brilliance, purity, and power.

I recall how impressed I was as a youth by Hawthorne's story of Rappaccini's daughter. Dr. Rappaccini, a botanist, nourished his beautiful daughter, Beatrice, on poisons, so that she, invulnerable, could aid him in his experiments with dangerous plants. Eventually she noted that she could kill insects by simply breathing upon them. Then of course she fell in love, but dared not approach nor kiss her loved one. This was a horrible story to me. I think of this description of Rappaccini's daughter, Beatrice, almost everytime I read apocalyptic statements that Christ will slay his enemies with the breath of his lips. I am convinced now that this should be taken metaphorically. His power over his enemies—those who oppose the will and purposes of the Lord—will be absolute. Those who oppose Christ's style of life, his demand for justice, mercy, compassion, and liberation cannot endure. Their day will end in defeat. They themselves will be defeated. Death will claim them and their purposes. But the statement that Jesus will achieve victory by blowing his breath upon them must be taken figuratively, not literally. We think of the lifegiving breath of God as envisioned by Ezekiel and pray: "Breathe on me breath of God, fill me with life anew." We need his spirit upon us.

HOW DOES ONE GET CLOSE TO GOD?

We should ask the question: How does a person get close to God? How do you get close to God? Does a person come closest to God when he climbs Mt. Everest, 29,300 feet above sea level? Recently I was flying in a plane at 31,300 feet above sea level—2,300 feet higher than Mt. Everest. There were many people on that plane who surely were not close to God. Some were filled with spirits—but not the Spirit of God! They had no awareness of the presence of God, yet they were higher than any person who has climbed Mt. Everest. Do those who fly to the moon get closer to God simply because they are 240,000 miles higher in the heavens? The point we must make clear is: God is Spirit! Altitude has nothing to do with closeness to God. It is attitude, not altitude, that brings a sense of the presence of God. God can be experienced everywhere.

I can recall my experience of deep religious emotion when I listened to the report that one of our American astronauts partook of the Lord's Supper as his spacecraft circled the moon for the first time. His pastor had made prior arrangements that this astronaut with his family and pastor—some 240,000 miles away—would commune together at the same time with the Risen Lord. And Christ, the Risen Lord, was at both places at the same time.

God is not localized in one place, but is omnipresent—he is everywhere. Our religious problem is to be sensitive to that presence which is always with us. Time and space are irrelevant in matters of relationship with God. God is on his throne—perhaps we ought to say that God is on his thrones, for he is enthroned in the hearts of people. The heart (*lebh* in Hebrew) was considered the seat of thought and motivation. To enthrone God in our hearts is to make him and his purposes the authority for our decision-making in all matters— political, domestic, international, economic, and personal. We need to fulfill the song "Come into my heart, come in today, come in to stay, come into my heart Lord Jesus." God wants to be a participant in the decisions of our lives. Oh yes, God is very near. He wants us to recognize him as near and to open our lives to his purposes and designs for a better human world.

THE ASCENSION
AND THE KINGDOM OF HEAVEN

Before turning to Daniel and Revelation, I would like to raise a theological issue concerning Jesus' ascension shortly after Pentecost. Affirming our modern view of the heavens and earth, what happened that day when Jesus ascended from their midst? Did he ascend to a third or seventh heaven and sit on the right hand of God? Remember our conclusions about the biblical world view of three to seven heavens.

In *Channels of His Spirit,* I suggested that we remember Paul's statement that Jesus was a spirit ("glorified") body after resurrection (I Corinthians 15). On the day of ascension, Jesus, the Christ who now was a glorified body left his disciples and apostles. He was no longer subject to the categories of time and space. So at any time the Risen Lord can be with a person on the moon and with his family in the USA and with Christians in Australia, Africa, and St. Albans all at the same time. Indeed, he could be with any and all living sons of God throughout his universe, for God is omnipresent.

When we say that God is omnipresent throughout his universe, we include not only the physical universe, but the areas which we have come to call heaven—"where the angels and archangels and all the company of heaven continually laud and magnify his glorious name." We have given up the notion of a physical heaven far up in the sky. But we still hold to the kingdom of heaven, which includes these persons of faith who have died before us as well as those who are living now— persons who have made their choice to be in Christ's kingdom.

Who then is in the kingdom of heaven? How does one enter that kingdom? A person becomes a citizen of that kingdom when he chooses to accept Jesus Christ as his Lord and Savior. Persons who choose to live the life-style of Jesus Christ, whose motives, purposes, attitudes are harmonized with those of Christ are already members of the kingdom of heaven. Death is not the point at which one enters the kingdom of heaven. It is during our lives that we make the choice as to whose kingdom we will identify our lives, our money, our time, our talents, our prayers. The time of decision-making is the time of entering the kingdom of heaven.

Where is the kingdom of heaven? Jesus didn't point upward and say: it's on the third or seventh heaven. Jesus did say: the kingdom of God is within you. The kingdom is among you. The kingdom of God is around you—it is in your relationships with persons and with God. God seeks persons whose attitudes and purposes reflect his own, those as seen in Jesus, and those in the living Lord today. God seeks persons whose attitudes reflect the kind of relationship that Jesus had with people.

So heaven is not a physical place "up there." But it is very real. It is a spirit realm where persons who have chosen Christ as their Savior and as their Lord, as the authority for their lives, continue to live in his presence. Jesus promised that he would go and prepare a place for them, and that he would come and receive them unto himself. Countless thousands have had the experience of the Risen Lord who has come and received them in both this life and through the experience we call death.

JESUS CHRIST THE LORD REIGNS

We need to decide who governs our earth and our universe. It is my firm conviction that we and our earth are under the reign of God and his Christ, the Risen Lord, yesterday, today, and forevermore.

Yet millions of people today are being falsely taught that Satan rules our world. This contradicts the psalmist who affirmed, "The earth is the Lord's and the fullness thereof. . . . The cattle on a thousand hills are *his*." We may truly sing "This is my Father's world, I rest me in the thought."

Hal Lindsey, however, develops a nonbiblical cosmology that states: when Adam and Eve sinned in Eden, Adam "forfeited to Satan his authority to rule the world. At that point, the arch-enemy of God legally took over the dominion of this earth."[1] The devil's legal document to earth turns out to be *mirabile dictu,* the scroll with seven seals mentioned in Revelation 5:1. Rather, the scroll with seven seals deals with judgments of God on the sins of man, not Satan.

But never mind, it will all come out in lily white purity when Michael, the archangel, stakes out a claim for possession of planet earth for Jesus. The archangel planted one foot on the sea and another foot on the land and raised his right hand to the heavens in a signal of conquest! The angel held a small open book in his left hand. This book turns out to be the title deed to the earth. The angel is making his "claim to the earth on behalf of Jesus Christ."[2] (This sounds like an account of explorers discovering America in the name of their king.)

This incredible view holds that while Satan held legal documents for earth, sinful, demonic-dominated mankind sought nobly to find God. In those terrible pre-Calvary days God loved his enemies; but after his Son died on the cross God's love turned to his friends (believers, the converts). What a strange effect Calvary had on God! God "who so loved the world" and also loved his enemies turned this great love from his enemies to his friends. In pre-Calvary days God's love reached out to sinners; but now, in post-Calvary days, God's love "floods believers who have all been washed from their sins and clothed with Christ's robes of righteousness."[3]

We cannot help but ask: Did the nature of God change at Calvary? Did the nature of God (love, justice, omniscience, etc.) change at Calvary? Who is the target audience of God's love? Hal Lindsey writes that God's love turned from loving enemies to loving his friends. Strangely, Jesus taught us to love our enemies. Are we to do and love that which God doesn't do and doesn't love? "For if you love those who love you, what reward have you? Do not even the tax collectors do the same?" (Matthew 5:46). Does Jesus correct and teach God how and whom to love? Absurdity, of course. So we refuse such theologizing, deny Lindsey's claims, and return to a firmer foundation of Christian faith!

No, God has not forsaken earth. He does not live far off in some remote heaven. He does not come on clouds to pay an occasional visit to planet earth, as Lindsey suggests.[4]

Jesus Christ does not have to wait for a millenium or two to reign. The Lord Jesus reigns now. The Apostle Paul emphasized that at the Resurrection "God has put all things in subjection under his feet" and that "he must reign until he has put all his enemies under his feet" (I Corinthians 15:25, 27).

The reign of the Lord includes our present age. The Risen Lord, reigning now, is as near as the door of our hearts. "Behold I stand at the door and knock; if any one hears my voice and opens the door, I will come in to him and eat with him, and he with me" (Revelation 3:20).

So I affirm the present lordship of Christ, whose reign was inaugurated at the time God raised him from the tomb and exalted him to be next to him in authority. This is the meaning of the often-used word *parousia:* the presence or coming. Christ comes now to us. We are aware of his presence at the door of our hearts (where intellect, morality, and will are lodged). Come Lord Jesus now, not a decade or century from now, but at this moment into my life.

No, Jesus Christ, the Risen and Reigning Lord is not seated on a physical throne up in heaven. He is involved in the redemption of persons today! I think it is time for Christians to look more carefully for those places where God is working in our day—that is, where God is enthroned. Moses could see that God was concerned about oppression—and lo, God was there! I think the Risen Lord is still as concerned as was the physical Jesus about the hungry, the naked, the oppressed. Take time to look for his divine activity in our world of human relations.

PROPHECY AND APOCALYPSE

We must distinguish between and affirm the value of both prophecy and apocalypse. God speaks through both channels of his Spirit.

Prophecy is an Old Testament word. I accept the definition of a prophet as given by the late Dr. Robert Pfeiffer of Harvard. He pointed out that the word prophet comes from the verb bo, to enter. The passive of that verb is "to be entered." A prophet is one who is entered (by the mind, attitudes, disposition of God). Thus a prophet "prophesies" as he relates what he understands the mind, attitudes, hopes, purposes of God are for mankind.

Thus Amos would say: "Thus saith the Lord: Let justice flow like a mighty river and righteousness like a mighty stream!" He declared God was concerned about justice in the courts of law in the land, justice in the market place, and honor and righteousness among nations. This is prophecy at its best. It involves man in God's hopes, dreams, and purposes for the world in which persons live.

What is a prophet? The Greek word *prophetes,* a translation of the Hebrew *nabi,* tends to emphasize the future, foretelling events of the future. This is but a small part or function of a prophet. The Hebrew word for prophet *(nabi)* is one who speaks forth, rather than foretells the future for God. Filled with God's attitudes and purposes the prophet speaks forth.

Apocalypse means hidden, hence deals with mysterious things, such as peculiar symbols (horned beasts, sealed documents, four horsemen).

The first full apocalypse is found in Daniel, written around 167-166 B.C. It was written to encourage the faithful Jew to maintain loyalty to God and their faith at all times and at all costs. Apocalypse are tracts for the faithful who live in periods of persecution, disillusionment, and apparent impotency to do anything to change terrible conditions. The apocalyptist, contrary to the prophets, does not call for involvement in society or in politics or in political structures. It considers the times so bad that only divine intervention can do any good. So apocalypse is the opposite of the prophetic stance.

One need only compare Daniel (both the stories, chapters 1,

3, 6, and visions) with Amos or Isaiah to see the difference. Isaiah spoke to the king against engaging in entangling alliances or being dependent on any one nation. The prophet sought to be involved with God in changing society. The prophet was a change agent, a catalyst.

The apocalyptist (as with the writer of Daniel or Revelation) seeks to encourage loyalty in the inner life of faith rather than overt action. Apocalypse encourages and challenges the faithful to loyalty to God, stedfastness in maintaining rituals, and trust in the Lord of history whose purposes will ultimately be victorious over the evil designs of persecutors.

We can affirm both prophecy and apocalypse in their basic concerns: (1) We affirm the need to participate with God in seeing that justice prevails in our world, that the hungry, naked, ill housed, and imprisoned find fulfillment. (2) We affirm that God is the Lord of history. (3) We affirm that Jesus is the Christ, the Risen Lord, and comes whenever we call on his name. We affirm that the parousia (the presence) is with us. We affirm the realization, the experience of Jesus' promise,. "Lo I will be with you always."

But we must read carefully, study scholarly commentaries, use Bible dictionaries, and meditate deeply as we read apocalyptic literature. The next part of this essay illustrates approaches that will help the reader in the study of this type of biblical literature.

On December 25, 165 B.C., a great event took place in Palestine. The event was the declaration of independence for the Jews. The Maccabees, a loyal and dedicated Jewish family, led a rebellion against the Greek authorities. This rebellion brought the Jews political independence for the first time since King Nebuchadnezzar had defeated and devastated Judah (586 B.C.) and took thousands of their people captive to Babylonia. The event was and is today celebrated by the feast of lights (Hannukah).

For over four centuries the Jews were ruled by foreign

powers. As such they were subject to the decrees ordered by foreign leaders. During this 523-year period (586-63 B.C.) they had felt the military heel of Babylonia, Media, Persia, and Greece on their daily lives. Who were these foreign countries, and who were their leaders?

Media was a small country north of Babylonia. Though a small country her great king (Cyaxares) led his well-trained military forces against the weakened giant Assyria and destroyed the beautiful yet infamous Nineveh in 612 B.C. We remember the Medes for their strict obedience to their state laws—so much so that even today we refer to the unchangeable laws of the Medes and the Persians.

Babylonia, at the southern end of the Tigris and Euphrates Rivers, resurrected the great ancient empire in 625 B.C. Two of their kings are well known to Bible students and will be readily recognized in this list of their four major kings: Nabopolasser (625-605 B.C.), Nebuchadrezzar (605-561 B.C.), Nabonidus, and his son, the regent, Belshazzar (555-538 B.C.). Belshazzar is remembered for the famous banquet during which the hand writing on the wall appeared (Daniel 5). The land of Judah knew only too well the harsh Babylonian hands of oppression, either as captive-slaves in Babylon or as heavily-taxed and militarily burdened citizens in Judah.

Succeeding the empires of Media and Babylon was Persia. The prophet Isaiah-of-Baylon (540 B.C.) thought so highly of the new Persian King Cyrus that he called him "the anointed of the Lord." He was indeed a most unusual military ruler. Cyrus conquered many nations including Lydia with its fabulously rich King Croesus; he bloodlessly captured Babylon by changing the course of the Euphrates so his soldiers could enter the capitol city on the old river bed that ran through the city. Cyrus decreed that all captives of all wars up to his time were free to return to their native lands. Furthermore, they could take their gods and religious appointments (such as golden bowls, incense burners, etc.) with them. This decree applied also to the Jews, some of whom finally returned to Judah to rebuild the destroyed temple (ca. 520 B.C.). Little wonder the prophet gave Cyrus the title of Messiah (Isaiah 45:1).

Cyrus was succeeded by Persian kings who were primarily interested in war and the domination of other countries. One of the great Persian kings was Xerxes I, who is remembered still by Greeks for his unique crossing of the Hellespont. In order to cross from Turkey into Europe, Xerxes had two pontoon bridges constructed. The Phoenician ship builders constructed 674 ships. They were lashed together side by side, with bows pointed upstream so they would face the currents flowing westward from the Black Sea and face the winds blowing in from the Aegean. Thousands of cedar planks (covered with dirt to calm skittish cavalry) were placed on the decks of the ships. In 480 B.C. Xerxes crossed the pontoon bridge in a chariot drawn by nine matched Nicaean horses. Two hundred thousand men crossed—taking seven days according to Herodotus. Judah (with the rest of the world) experienced fear at the Persian military genius and power.

In 331 B.C. Alexander the Great brought to Judah the fourth foreign power since 586 B.C. This Greek military genius sought to capture all nations on earth in order to make the world one. He wanted one language, one culture, one economic structure, one government (Greek controlled, of course). But his dream died aborning due to his early death in 323 B.C. Alexander the Great had hoped his infant son would succeed him. But due to his ambitious generals Alexander divided his empire into four parts with each general ruling a fourth of his empire (I Maccabees 1; Daniel 3:21-22):

1. The homeland (Macedonia and Greece) went to Antigonus;

2. Pergamum and much of Asia Minor went to Lysimachus;

3. The rest of Asia Minor and Syria went to Seleuchus;

4. Egypt, with Palestine, went to Ptolemy.

The people of Judah experienced the consequences of jealous rivalry between the last two rulers (Seleuchus of Syria and Ptolemy of Egypt). The armies of these two forces swaggered back and forth over the land of Judah leaving countless dead and terrible devastation. Finally the Syrians defeated Egypt, and thus Syria ruled Palestine (198 B.C.).

Just two decades later (175 B.C.) the Seleucid ruler Antiochus Epiphanes IV came to Judah with the intent of hellenizing ("greekizing") Judah. He was determined that all nations, including Judah, would have one culture and one religion.

It was under the rule of this Seleucid king that Judah won its political freedom in 165 B.C. But their freedom, the first in 523 years, lasted for only a century, at which time Pompey, the Roman, conquered Palestine (63 B.C.) and placed the land and people under the rule and authority of the Roman eagle.

Antiochus Epiphanes sought to make all citizens in his kingdom embrace the same religion, making the Greek god Zeus the deity of all. So Antiochus Epiphanes outlawed Judaism. He ordered that no one should observe the Jewish religious rituals; no one should read the sacred scriptures; there should be no festivals, no observance of Yom Kippur, no feast of tabernacles, no Pentecost, no circumcision of the new born sons. But to accept the decree outlawing their faith was one thing that many Jews could not do.

King Antiochus Epiphanes IV wrote a letter to all the kingdom. He decreed (in 168 B.C.) that each Jew should give up his religious customs and observance of religious festivals. First Maccabees, chapter one, recounts the events:

> Now on the fifteenth day of Chislev [December 25, 168 B.C.] Antiochus Epiphanes erected a desolating sacrilege on the altar of burnt offering. [Zeus was placed in the Holy of Holies.] They also built altars in the surrounding cities of Judea and burned incense at the doors of the houses and in the streets. The books of the law

[the Pentateuch] which they found they tore to pieces and they burned them with fire. Where the book of the covenant was found in the possession of any one or if any one adhered to the law, the decree of the king condemned him to death. . . . According to the decree they put to death the women who had their children circumcised, and their families and those who circumcised them; and they hung the infants from their mother's necks. But many in Israel stood firm and they were resolved in their hearts not to eat the unclean food (1:54-58, 60-64). [As with Daniel, in the stories of chapters 1, 3, 4, 5, and 6, many preferred death to disloyalty.]

DANIEL—STORIES AND VISIONS OF LOYALTY AND HOPE

The above is the historical background which inspired the book of Daniel to be written. Note the way in which the book of Daniel was written to meet this terrible outlawing of their faith. First, the stories of Daniel's unyielding loyalty to the kosher (pure) food he ate and loyalty to festivals and prayers—regardless of what happened—even to being tossed into a den of lions or into a fiery furnace. Daniel loyally said: "Our God whom we serve is able to deliver us. . . . But if not, be it known unto you, o king, that we will not serve your gods or worship the golden image you have set up" (3:17-18). Imagine how these stories encouraged faithful Jews to be stedfast and loyal even unto death.

Besides several stories (chapters 1, 3, 5, 6) in the book of Daniel, there are also visions, whose purpose was to encourage the discouraged and brokenhearted. These visions are the apocalyptic parts of the book of Daniel that we will study. [Portions of apocalyptical writings appear in the writings of a number of the prophets, such as in Ezekiel and Zechariah.]

Daniel describes a great image in the form of a man. Daniel 2:32 reads "The head of this image was of fine gold; its breast and arms of silver, its belly and thighs of bronze, its legs of iron, its feet partly of iron and partly of clay."

Daniel proceeds to identify the head of the image (made of gold) as Babylon whose king, Nebuchadnezzar, had the dream Daniel is interpreting (2:38). The breast and arms of silver represent Media. The belly and thighs of bronze represent Persia; the legs of iron and clay represent Greece (ruled by Alexander the Great until his death). Verse 41 refers to the two legs as the divided kingdom—one leg referring to the Seleucid dynasty that ruled Syria and Palestine and the other leg of the huge image referring to the Ptolemies who ruled in Egypt. [The vision in Daniel 8:20-21 identifies these same four nations.]

This apocalyptic vision firmly declared that the nations were doomed. The golden age of Babylon, the silver age of Media, the bronze age of Persia, the iron age of Greece with its mixture of iron and potters clay of the Seleucid kings were at their end. The great nations were falling apart. Antiochus Epiphanes IV would soon crumble. God would soon reinstate Israel as the ruling nation.

Daniel 7 tells of a vision about four beasts. The first is a lion that has two eagle's wings. The second is a bear which has three ribs in its teeth. And the third beast is a leopard with four wings of a bird and four heads. Then a fourth ferocious beast,

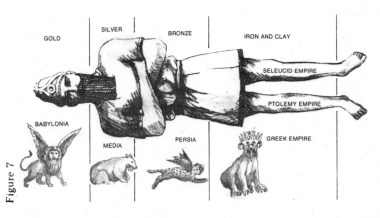

Figure 7

a huge and wild animal appears. He has ten horns. Note the
numerology inherent in the scheme of four animals: the lion
has the number two—two eagle wings and two feet; the bear
has the number three—three ribs in its teeth; the leopard has
four wings and four heads; the fourth beast 10 horns (five
horns each for Seleucids and Ptolemys)! Numerology is a part
of apocalyptic literary form. In the book of Revelation there is a
beast with seven heads, and ten crowns.

What in the world do all these beasts mean? First, I want to
say very clearly, there never were such creatures that lived.
There are no such creatures today. I have seen paintings and
sculptured beasts like those which Daniel described in the
museums of Baghdad, Istanbul, Paris, and London. The art
work is magnificent. But Daniel is not interested in art here.
He is using these beasts to represent movements of nations
and history.

Daniel 7 declares through his vision of four beasts that the
end of the mighty four nations is near. Mighty Babylon,
Media, Persia, and the Greek empires have devoured one
another. Now God will intervene to stop the Greek (Seleucid)
leader, Antiochus Epiphanes, who rules over Syria and Palestine. Daniel's vision includes four great beasts that came up
out of the sea, each different from the other. The first was a
lion that had two eagle's wings. But its wings were plucked
and the lion was lifted up from the ground and made to stand
on two feet like a man. The lion symbolized Babylon. The
second beast was like a bear, it had three ribs in its mouth.
This symbolized Media. The third beast was Persia, symbolized by a leopard with four wings of a bird on his back; and
the beast had four heads and dominion was given to it. After
this Daniel saw a fourth beast: "terrible and dreadful, and
exceedingly strong." Daniel writes

> And it had iron teeth, it devoured and broke in pieces, and
> stamped the residue with its feet. I considered the horns [the ten
> Greek kings following the death of Alexander the Great], and

behold, there came up among them another horn, a little one,
before which three of the first horns were plucked by the roots
(Daniel 7:8).

The strong little horn was Antiochus Epiphanes IV, whom
we read about in I Maccabees 1. It was he who outlawed
Judaism, killed anyone who was found reading the law, the
Torah. He ordered the death of any circumcised boy and that
the infant be hung around its mother's neck. "Behold in this
little horn [Antiochus Epiphanes, ca. 168 B.C.] were eyes like
the eyes of a man and a mouth speaking great things." Daniel
was saying clearly to his generation: these kings aren't the
enduring kings. There is a greater king, the king of kings;
there is a Lord of lords. There is only one king of kings and
there is only one Lord of lords, and it surely isn't Antiochus
Epiphanes! Daniel was pleading, "You who understand, listen
to me. Don't give in to these rulers and kings and their demands. There is only one Lord, and history is in his hands. I
call you to courage; I call you to loyalty; I call you to maintain
your religious faith."

I want to call special attention to the fourth beast. This
terrible beast has ten horns. In the book of Revelation this
beast is called the anti-Christ. But in Daniel's day it had a very
different and specific meaning. I want to make that point
clear. I ask you to realize that these beasts represented kings
and events of Daniel's day. They do not refer to events of our
day. I think it is a woeful abuse of the book of Daniel to try to
find who or what the ten horns are referring to in our day. Hal
Lindsey writes that the ten horns are the ten nations in the
common market of Europe.[5] This is gross error and a misread-
ing of Daniel. To read your own ideas into a text is eisegesis
rather than exegesis. Daniel 7 was talking about the Seleucid
king of that day (168 B.C.). We ought to realize that Daniel 7 is
a tremendous message of enthusiasm; it is a book calling for
faith, loyalty, and courage to a people who lived under the
cruel persecution of the Seleucids. The little horn was An-

tiochus Epiphanes. The ten horns were the ten Greek kings succeeding Alexander the Great.

Daniel's vision changed to the scene of the heavenly assize. There were twenty-four thrones plus one where the Ancient of Days (God) had taken his seat. His raiment was white as snow and the hair of his head was pure wool. A thousand thousands served him. To "serve" God meant, as in the German word *gottesdienst,* to worship him. A million beings, a thousand thousand, and ten thousand times ten thousand—a hundred million stood before him. The court sat in judgment, and the books were opened. Daniel writes, "I looked then because of the sound of the great words which the horn [Antiochus Epiphanes] was speaking. And as I looked the beast was slain, and its body was destroyed and given over to be burned with fire." Daniel declared in writing to his persecuted countrymen: Only God, the living God rules ultimately.

> As for the other three beasts their dominion was taken away, . . . and behold, with the clouds of heaven there came one like a son of man, and he came to the Ancient of Days and was presented before him. And to him was given dominion and glory and kingdom, that all peoples, nations, and languages should serve him; his dominion is an everlasting dominion.

In Daniel the "son of man" refers to the saints of Judaism— Israel. It was II Ezra of the apocrypha that later identified the "son of man" with the Messiah. This same identification is picked up in the book of Revelation.

Well, our brief introduction to Daniel has illustrated the what and how of apocalyptic literature. In summary, in the days of Antiochus Epiphanes, the author of Daniel was writing so that the authorities who read his document would think that the poor writer ought to be put in a pit with other insane persons. Similarly, John, writing on the island of Patmos, wrote in a literary form so that the authorities did not know what he was saying. But his readers had no difficulty understanding. Each writer was writing quite clearly for the readers of his day about conditions of their time. The same kind of literary device was used by Eszra at the time Titus desecrated the temple and destroyed Jerusalem, A.D. 70. Eszra used symbols for his message of encouragement too. His readers understood.

REVELATION—LETTERS FROM JOHN TO HIS CHURCHES

John the Elder used the same kind of religious literature, apocalypse, when he wrote Revelation. The times were very similar. The Emperor Domitian (ca. A.D. 90-95) was persecuting gentile Christians. Domitian learned that his niece, Domitilla was a Christian, so he exiled her and murdered her husband (named Theophilus) who was heir to the throne of the Roman Empire. These acts were a part of the persecution of the early church by Rome because Christians dared to openly embrace the faith of Jesus Christ. We cannot but wonder what the Empire would have been like if Theophilus had become the emperor and had been won to Christ as Luke attempted to do when he wrote his gospel and addressed his "Book of Acts" to "Excellent Theophilus!"

Gentile Christians, as with Jews under Antiochus Epiphanes and Titus (A.D. 70, when Jerusalem was destroyed by the Roman armies), were being persecuted for their faith. Christians throughout the world were ordered to worship the image of the Caesar; if they refused, they were denied the right to purchase food and clothing in the market places and to probate wills. Some were thrown into the gladiatorial arena to be slowly tortured by wild beasts.

So John, Bishop of Asia Minor, exiled some sixty miles south of his beloved Asia Minor on the desolate island of Patmos, decided to write a document of encouragement to the faithful. John wanted to encourage his beloved Christians to maintain loyalty to Christ at all costs. He wanted to tell them that Domitian (the popular revived or resurrected hero) was not a god. Caesar worship was wrong and would soon come to a bitter end. God himself would see to it! John knew he would have to write treasonable statements. In order to get a message out of Patmos, his document would have to be so written that only the faithful would understand. So John wrote an apocalypse. The military would consider him insane!

So first he wrote seven letters to the seven churches of Asia Minor, those founded for the most part by the apostle Paul. The letters were written to churchmen of A.D. 95 for their comfort, inspiration, and encouragement. Each church read its letter and both rejoiced and acted on John's recommendations. It is a gross error to assign each of the seven letters to various churches during the past nineteen hundred years of church history as some Bible students do. For example, it is said by some that the Ephesus period was a prophecy concerning the first century church; the Smyrna period the church of the Church Fathers (A.D. 100-300); the Pergamum period from Constantine to Boniface (A.D. 300-600); the Thyatira period from Boniface to the Reformation and the Decline of the Papacy (A.D. 600-1500); the Sardis period from the Reformation to the peace of Westphalia (1500-1700); the last two Philadelphia and Laodicea periods lead up to our own age— hence to the time for the Rapture, which is due any time now. We are at the end of the last church period as proven by the return of some 10 percent of the Jews to Israel. There is not one good solid reason for such an exegesis. This suggests then that we are in eisegesis again—where the interpreter brings his own ideas and superimposes them on scripture. Hal Lindsey is one interpreter who incorrectly assumes that the letters to the seven churches are prophecies for seven periods of church history. His scheme is almost identical to the one above, but this is an abuse, a terrible misuse of scripture. These letters had nothing to do with the periods of church history just referred to. The seven letters were written for the one period when John wrote, A.D. 95, during the persecutions of Emperor Domitian of Rome. They were personal letters to specific young congregations in Asia Minor, not in Europe and certainly not to the United States.

John wrote for the people of his day who were being forced by Roman priests of the Emperor cult to bow and worship the image of Caesar Domitian. After they had worshiped, the priests placed an indelible mark on their hand or on their forehead. This mark was given after they had worshiped, not before. With the mark they could then make purchases in the market places and could notarize documents—such as deeds for the sale of a house, etc. Without the marks they were in dire circumstances.

THE TWO BEASTS OF REVELATION

In this brief statement about the apocalypse called Revelation, let me comment on several verses from Revelation 13: "I saw a beast rising out of the sea, with ten horns and seven heads, with ten diadems upon its horns and a blasphemous name upon its heads." (What blasphemous name? Perhaps Augustus, as in Augustus Caesar, for Augustus means divine. Augustus (divine) Caesar. This is blasphemy, since no Caesar is God.) This is similar to the blasphemous name "Epiphanes" (God manifest) noted in our study of Daniel.

Figure 8

The beast of Revelation 13 is a composite of the four beasts of Daniel 7. We read (Revelation 13:2-8), "And the beast that I saw was like a leopard, its feet were like a bear's, and its mouth was like a lion's mouth. And to it the dragon gave his power and his throne and great authority. One of its heads seemed to have a mortal wound but its mortal wound was healed, and the whole earth followed the beast with wonder. Men worshiped the dragon, for he had given his authority to the beast, and they worshiped the beast." And the beast was given a mouth uttering haughty and blasphemous words, and it was allowed to exercise authority for forty-two months. (That is, "time and two times and half a time"—three and one-half years—this too is a timing device from Daniel.) "It [the beast] opened its mouth to utter blasphemies against God, blaspheming his name and his dwelling. Also it was allowed to make war on the saints and to conquer them. And authority was given it over every tribe and people and tongue and nation, and all who dwell on earth will worship it."

How shall we understand this beast and its actions? Keeping in mind that the writer, John, was writing for his own Christian friends in Asia Minor, we can identify the beast with the Roman Empire (under the rule of Emperor Domitian, ca. A.D. 95). The seven heads refer to the seven emperors who called themselves augustus (divine). The names of these seven august (divine) ones are: (1) Tiberius; (2) Caligula (who was probably insane); (3) Claudius; (4) Nero (who committed suicide; many Romans claimed that when he stabbed his throat he died but that he would revive and rule again. Hence the claim: Nero Redivivus. Many thought he had come alive in Domitian. John wrote that one of the seven heads of the beast had been mortally wounded, but had revived. This refers to Nero who died and was believed to have revived and ruled through Domitian.); (5) Vespasian; (6) Titus; and (7) Domitian. There were three other emperors, Galba, Otho, and Vitellius, but they each ruled about three months and were never referred to as "augustus." So the seven Emperors listed above bore the blasphemous name augustus, and this word appeared on the seven heads of the beast. The ten crowns represented these seven august ones plus the three emperors who were not referred to as augustus. So the beast had ten crowns and seven heads, each of which had the blasphemous name augustus written on it.

As we read further beginning with chapter 13:11 we read that there was another, a second beast, which rose out of the earth: "It had two horns like a lamb and it spoke like a dragon. It exercises all the authority of the first beast in its presence, and makes the earth and its inhabitants worship the first beast, whose mortal wound was healed!"

Let me explain what I am convinced John meant by this second beast. It is the priesthood of the emperor worship of Rome (A.D. 95). Recall that the Asiarchs in Ephesus were priests of the cult of emperor worship. They joined Paul in his stand against the worship of Diana of Ephesus. The Asiarchs were not interested in Paul's faith. They wanted their own deities, the Roman emperors (the august Caesars), to be worshiped. Paul of course wanted the Lord, the Father of Jesus Christ to be worshiped, and he wanted Jesus to be accepted as the Risen Lord, the Messiah. What strange bedfellows: Paul and the Asiarchs.

John wrote that the second beast, such as the Asiarchs of Ephesus, "makes the earth and its inhabitants worship the first head, whose mortal wound was healed" (13:12). Nero, as popular belief held, had been revived in Domitian. So Domitian ("Nero Redivivus") is this "first head, whose mortal wound was healed." John writes that the second beast, the priests, "causes all, both small and great, both rich and poor, both free and slave, to be marked on the right hand or the forehead, so that no one can buy or sell unless he has the mark, that is the number of the beast or the number of its name. This calls for wisdom: Let him who has understanding

reckon the number of the beast, for it is a human number, its
number is six hundred and sixty six." (Revelation 13:16-18) If
you were a Hebrew Christian reading the book of Revelation
you would be reading from the Greek in which it was written
and be translating it into Aramaic (or Hebrew). As you translated the last phrase (vs. 17) from Greek into Aramaic you
would have read (or written) the name of Nero Caesar. For the
numbers 666 when written in Aramaic is קסר נרון (which
spells Neron Caesar). The Jews disliked the use of Arabic
numbers (1, 2, 3, etc.), so they used letters of their Hebrew
alphabet as numbers. Aramaic and Hebrew read from right to
left. Below is the way the number 666 would have been
written in Aramaic, the language in which Jesus spoke.

	ר	ס	ק		ן	ו	ר	נ
666 =	200	60	100		50	6	200	50
CAESAR, NERO	r	s	c		n	o	r	n

Several early manuscripts of Revelation omit the second "n"
in Neron which gives Nero, so the number 666 is reduced by
50 (the letter n) to the number 616. This would be the Hebrew
rather than Aramaic spelling for Nero Caesar. Aramaic, a
language almost identical to Hebrew, was the language Jesus
used in teaching and was the language used by Jews who
lived in Gentile lands. John very likely spelled Nero with two
N's (Neron, giving 666).

The number 666 refers to the historical period of A.D.
90-95—and specifically to Nero Caesar who was considered
"redivivus" (living again) in Domitian.

I am trying to say as firmly as possible that the number 666
does not refer to a man of the twentieth century nor to one in
the middle ages! It was in those terrible days of persecution of

Christians under Domitian (Nero Redivivus) that the number 666 applies. John clearly stated: It is a "human number," and it is the "number of the beast." Nero Caesar (living in Domitian) is the number 666. So John was writing his apocalypse to Christians of A.D. 95 to take courage and hold to their faith that Jesus was the Christ and their only Lord of life. John wrote in the style of the literature of apocalypse so that the Roman authorities, by whom he was imprisoned at Patmos, would not comprehend, yet his loved ones in the seven churches of Asia Minor would!

A MODERN MESSAGE VIA APOCALYPSE

I would like to tell a personal experience I had during World War II. Christians in Germany were being mocked by the question: Who reigns, Hitler or God? They asked: Is Hitler really the dictator who will establish a millenial kingdom? He did make that claim, didn't he? He had a messianic image of himself. I remember when our forces went to Dusseldorf. There was a German pastor of an Evangelishe Kirke to whose home I went at the orders of my colonel. I was to arrange for a worship service for our headquarters company. I was to tell that pastor what time we were to hold our services, and then he could set the hour of worship for their congregation accordingly. I remember knocking on the door, my driver remaining with our jeep out in front. When the German pastor saw my American uniform, he stood erect, clicked his heels together, and bowed his head without saying a word. He was saying nonverbally: I am among the conquered. What do you want of me? I asked if I could enter his home. He said: *bitte schön.* I immediately held out my hand and said: *"Du bist mein Bruder in Christos."* He smiled, and we clasped hands; and we were brothers in Christ!

Having set the hours of worship for Sunday's *gottesdienst,* we had a good chat together. The pastor told me that on several occasions the Gestapo had come to his worship service (gottesdienst). The Gestapo would come and sit in the first row because they wanted to know what Christian preachers were preaching about Hitler and the Third Reich.

The pastor told me that since the Gestapo sat directly in front of him at the service he realized that what he needed to do was to use some figures of speech that his congregation would understand, yet which the Gestapo would consider gibberish. So he told them an allegory about some strange beasts: About a bear and a lopsided leopard that had wings like a bird, about a lion with a little horn that spoke blasphemous words. The pastor told of the heavenly assize with the Ancient of Days sitting on his throne. He told how his hair was white, white as wool, and his eyes flashed like fire. He would destroy his enemies with his two-edged sword, his tongue! And the people said: Amen. The Gestapo thought: What a nut this preacher is! They left mystified by the sermon. The congregation left with courage to be loyal to God, whose purposes would ultimately prevail. Apocalypse in 1944 was a most helpful literary device. So it was also when John used it in A.D. 95.

John was saying to his parishioners of Asia Minor (A.D. 95) and to all who are truly persecuted for Christ's sake: "The beastial authorities have their day. They are not God, they are all very human, and their day will come to a close. God will bring their rule to an end inasmuch as God's own kingdom shall ultimately rule the world." John, true to the literature of apocalypse, assured the faithful that the kingdom of God would sometime become incarnate in the kingdoms of this world, or, conversely, the kingdoms of this world shall become the kingdoms of our Christ.

The book of Revelation begins with the state of things as they were, then moves to things as they are, and finally to things as they shall be (Revelation 1:1-19). The things that were include: "God made us a kingdom, priests to his God and Father . . . I am the Alpha and Omega." The things that are refers to the seven churches of A.D. 90-95—not to the groups of churches during the past eighteen hundred years as some incorrectly suggest. The seven churches of Asia Minor to whom John writes in Revelation were: Ephesus, Smyrna, Pergamos, Thyatira, Sardis, Philadelphia, and Laodicea. Then John spoke of what shall be ... but let us follow John's sequence: consider Revelation 4 and 5; then consider the "Rapture" followed by things that shall be.

JOHN'S CREATIVE USE OF HIS OLD TESTAMENT

John, the writer of Revelation, loved his Bible, the Old Testament. His visions are replete with the imagery and metaphors of the writings of both prophets and apocalypse. He not only made use of the beasts of Daniel's vision (with their ten crowns, horns, and blasphemous words printed on them) but also the imagery of the theophanies of great men like Moses, Elijah, Isaiah, and Ezekiel. John's literary art in Revelation is like that of a beautiful tapestry. One needs to give close attention to its threads to appreciate it. This is especially true in Revelation 4 and 5, where John displays his sensitivity to the great verbal artists who wrote before him. We might think of chapters 4 and 5 as a magnificent collage of Old Testament theophanies—times when God revealed himself uniquely to persons. John knew that the God who once revealed himself continues to do so. Let us look at these two chapters in Revelation which speak of the eternal realities in heaven.

John writes: "At once I was in the Spirit, and lo, a throne stood in heaven, with one seated on the throne!" John experienced the majesty, power, glory, wisdom, and honor of God Almighty. John undoubtedly sought ways of expressing his experience of being in the presence of God. John was expressing the inexpressible, uttering words about the ineffable.

There can be no doubt but that this great Christian mind was saturated with the faith and words of the men of God of Old Testament times.

Moses at Mt. Sinai experienced God's presence and heard God's call for him to come to the top of the mount: "On the morning of the third day there were thunders and lightnings, and a thick cloud upon the mountain, and a very loud trumpet blast, so that all the people who were in the camp trembled. . . . And as the sound of the trumpet grew louder and louder, Moses spoke, and God answered him in thunder" (Exodus 19:16, 19).

Four hundred years later Elijah, at Mt. Sinai, was told to stand on the mount.

> And behold, the Lord passed by, and a great and strong wind rent the mountains, and broke in pieces the rocks before the Lord, but the Lord was not in the wind; and after the wind an earthquake, but the Lord was not in the earthquake; and after the earthquake a fire, but the Lord was not in the fire; and after the fire a still small voice. And when Elijah heard it, he wrapped his face in his mantle (I Kings 19:11-13*b*).

A hundred years after Elijah's experience, Isaiah "saw the Lord sitting upon a throne, high and lifted up; and his train filled the temple. Above him stood the seraphim; each had six wings. . . . And one called to another and said: 'Holy, holy, holy is the Lord of hosts; the whole earth is full of his glory.' And the foundations of the thresholds shook at the voice of him who called, and the house was filled with smoke" (Isaiah 6:1-3).

Ezekiel, a little less than two hundred years later, while on the Chebar canal in Babylonia as an exile of war, experienced God's greatness and otherness too. As with Moses he experienced a stormy wind and a great cloud, with brightness round about it, and fire flashing forth continually (Ezekiel 1:4). With Isaiah he experienced living creatures (seraphim and cherubim) around the throne of God. Archaeologists have identified the cherubim from several locations. They were composite creatures, each having a head like a man, a body like a lion, wings like an eagle, and feet of an ox. In Isaiah's day these were the four gods of Assyrian religion: Nergal, a winged lion, symbolizing majesty; Marduk, a winged bull, symbolizing strength and power; Nebo, a human being, symbolizing intelligence; and Ninib, an eagle, symbolizing loftiness. God's throne was metaphorically upheld by the majesty, power, intelligence, and loftiness which had been falsely claimed for these Assyrian deities.

Ezekiel adds that the four creatures each had four faces: a lion, bull, eagle, and man. And these four four-faced creatures upheld a flaming chariot of God from whence came lightning. There were four wheels, with rims, which were full of eyes symbolizing omniscience. These creatures upheld the "likeness of a firmament, shining like crystal, spread out above their heads" (1:22). And "the sounds of their wings [was] like the sounds of many waters, like the thunder of the Almighty" (4:24). "And above the firmament over their heads there was the likeness of a throne, in appearance like sapphire; and seated above the likeness of a throne was a likeness as it were of a human form. . . . Such was the appearance of the likeness of the glory of the Lord" (Ezekiel 4:26, 28b).

With these ancient expressions of experiences of men with God, John artistically knit the passages together, adding to the scene of the heavenly assize the presence of the Risen Lord.

Turn to Revelation 4 and 5, and read these two chapters. Note how beautifully John used the ancient expressions to describe his experience too: He saw God seated on a throne. The rainbow, as in Ezekiel's experience, is the backdrop for the divine throne. Isaiah, Ezekiel, and John all knew that God was Spirit, so could not be physically seated on a throne—for they understood this is poetry, not prose. In this chapter John feels rather than thinks his faith. God reigns, God rules in majesty, loftiness, intelligence, and power as the King of kings in the kingdom of God. God is honored by the worship of the twenty-four elders "casting down their golden crowns upon the glassy sea." The cherubim are present and continue to sing: "Holy, holy, holy is the Lord God Almighty, who was and is and is to come." No one thinks of his own greatness or cleverness or intellectual ability or personal material wealth when in the presence of God!

Chapter 5 introduces the vision of the Redeemer, who alone is worthy to open the scroll which Daniel had sealed with seven seals (Daniel 12:4). The lion of the tribe of Judah, from the root of David (from whence came the Messiah, Jesus Christ), can open the scroll and its seven seals. The Messiah, who suffered as the sacrificial lamb, took the scrolls and prepared to read.

Then the participants in the heavenly assize sang a new song, saying:

> "Worthy art thou to take the scroll and to open its seals,
> for thou wast slain and by thy blood didst ransom men for God
> from every tribe and tongue and people and nation,
> and hast made them a kingdom and priests to our God,
> and they shall reign on earth" (Revelation 5:9-10).

You can almost hear John saying: I looked, and saw and heard thousands upon thousands singing: "Oh, for a thousand tongues to sing my great Redeemer's name!" And they sang: "Worthy is the Lamb who was slain to receive power and wealth and wisdom and might and honor and glory and blessing." And the four creatures around the throne said amen.

Handel's *Messiah* seeks to express this hymn of praise: Worthy is the Lamb who brought liberation, cleansing, loyalty, certainty, hope, and victory! John wrote that voices of heaven, earth, and under the earth and on the sea joined with the cherubic choirs as they sang: "To him who sits upon the throne and to the Lamb be blessing and honor and glory and might for ever and ever." And the elders fell down and worshiped (Revelation 5:13-14).

THE RAPTURE

Some popular writers on Revelation and some radio preachers state that the "Rapture" will soon take place. The Rapture refers to those Christians who have died in Christ who will be resurrected and join living Christians, all of whom will be caught up together in the clouds with Jesus. "And so we shall always be with the Lord" (Thessalonians 4:15-18). Lindsey calls the Rapture "the Great Snatch," since only believers will be "snatched" up leaving disbelievers behind on earth to endure the seven years of torment and wars of the Tribulation. Perhaps you have seen the bumper stickers on cars "In case of the Rapture this car is unmanned." I saw an interesting bumper with that slogan on the left side of the bumper; on the right side was "God is my copilot." Lindsey writes that "clouds are frequently the vehicle in which heavenly visits were paid to this planet by God" (see Psalm 104:3; Isaiah 19:1).[6]

A film entitled *The Thief That Comes in the Night* portrays the fear, anxiety, and horror of small children whose parents suddenly disappear "up into the clouds" to be with Jesus. The film calls for decisions to accept Jesus as Christ and Savior. It is quite illustrative of apocalyptic literature and methodology of winning converts. It makes no prophetic demands for seeking to establish justice in the market place or in the courts of law or better housing or employment available to all. I have watched a dozen junior-high boys and girls go to the altar "to accept Jesus" because of fear that their parents would leave them behind on earth. They were converted through fear rather than through acceptance of the love of Jesus Christ, our Risen Lord. The film is based on the false concept that the world belongs to Satan and that God has purposely absented himself from this earth. The film overlooks the claim of John 3:16 that God so loved the world; or that the "earth is the Lord's and the fullness thereof." The Rapture is Pauline (I Thessalonians 4:15-18), and it has erroneously been inserted into the book of Revelation where it was not described at all by John.

A very popular writer in this field has set the date for the Rapture. The date is set by the key date of May 15, 1948, when Israel became a nation, and when the Jews (less than 10 percent) returned to Israel. By adding one generation (forty years) to 1948 the writer sets 1988 as the approximate time for the Second Coming of Jesus.[7] This is the current date being scheduled for the Rapture—the date when the believers will be drawn from earth into the clouds in the same way a huge electromagnetic device pulls iron to it. (I might remark that in the setting of dates for the Second Coming "there is no end.")

But here is the problem: Do we not affirm the parousia, the presence of the Risen Lord, Jesus Christ, with us *now*? Was not his promise of nineteen hundred years ago "Lo, I am with you always even unto the end of the age" fulfilled through the centuries—hundreds and hundreds and thousands and thousands of times? If Christ the Risen Lord is with us now, what gain is there in being drawn up into the sky to be with him—except of course to escape having to live with unbelievers? I align myself with the fourth Gospel in its strong argument that the Risen Lord has already come, and is with us now. He came when he was resurrected; and was known as free from time and space at the ascension. The danger of waiting for a far off time for his calling us to the skies is the danger of not even knowing that we should be aware of his presence now.

Affirming the Lord's presence and his urgent continuing challenge for us to be involved in his purposes—sharing the good news to the poor, liberating the oppressed, helping the blind to see—let us become channels of his Spirit now. As we accept him as Lord of our life (in all areas of our life) we work with him in proclaiming and establishing the kingdom of God on earth as it is in heaven.

THINGS THAT ARE TO BE (ESCHATOLOGY)

John in Revelation, having written about things that were and then about things that are, finally portrays the things that are to be.

These future events include opening of the scroll which is sealed with the seven seals (Revelation 6:1-8:5); the blowing of the seven trumpets (Revelation 8:7-11:19); significant personages (Revelation 12:1-13:18, which includes the two beasts we have discussed); the seven bowls or vials (Revelation 15:1-16:21); the seven dooms (Revelation 17:1-20:15); then the millennium (the second coming of Jesus) followed by the new heaven and the new earth. It seems ludicrous to me to hear (via popular apocalyptists) that the scroll with seven seals is Satan's legal document for ownership of earth, where he reigns in demonic glee as he continues to win souls for hell. [8]

There is a great deal of speculation these days about the Second Coming of Jesus. It is said he will come at any time. So be ready. Signs along the highway for thirty years have read "Prepare to meet thy God." I am deeply troubled with these statements inasmuch as I am convinced that the Risen Lord is already here. I have asked myself hundreds of times what the Heavenly Christ at a second coming would do that he is not already doing as the Risen Lord who is with us now? Are his purposes the same? Are his methods the same, or are they different? Is Jesus Christ the same yesterday, today, and forever? I am convinced that he is! I'm counting on the stability of his character and his purposes and methods.

One major question persists in my mind as I ponder the

second coming of Jesus. It has to do with his temptations
when he knew for the first time at baptism that he was the
Messiah, the Christ. For forty days and nights he was in the
wilderness working through the various Jewish concepts as to
what the Messiah would be like, what he would do, what his
goals were and how he would achieve them. In Jesus' day
there were many views as to what the Messiah would do and
what he would be like.

Jesus refused and denied the Messianic nature, goals, and
methods of each and every religious party of his day. He
turned down the Pharisee's way of obedience to both written
and oral law as the way of bringing in the kingdom of God in
the daily life of persons. Jesus refused the Sadducees' priestly
emphasis on careful regulations and observances of festivals
(such as Passover, Pentecost, Day of Atonement). Likewise he
refused to be the Messiah of the Zealots who assumed the
Messiah would form a great army and force the Roman army
of occupation out of Palestine. Jesus denied the methods for
the coming of the Messiah as held by the Essenes at Qumran
who thought the Messiah would come in the clouds of heaven
at the head of a massive military force to conquer by violence
and death and claim the physical throne of David and rule
with a rod of iron. Jesus refused them all. And the Risen Lord
still refuses this popular, but mistaken view of the living God's
Messiah—Jesus Christ, our Lord.

During the temptations in the wilderness Jesus sought the
will of God as to what kind of Messiah God [not the religious
parties of his day] wanted him to be. It was clear at the
Baptism that Jesus was the Son of God, the suffering servant,
the holy one, the elect—the Messiah. But it also became clear
during the forty days following his baptism that Jesus could
not accept any of the popular views of the Messiah. Instead, he
took the insights of Isaiah 42 and 52, the suffering servant, as
the key to the nature, methods, and purposes of God's Messiah.

Jesus refused to be the kind of Messiah who would rule by force, convert by coercion, and sit on the throne of David in Jerusalem forcing all other nations to bow down and serve him and the chosen people of Israel. Jesus refused this temptation. It was not, and is not, God's way of winning converts; nor the Lord's way of expressing his authority. Christ's way is the way of persuasion not coercion, of suffering for others not slaying them with the breath of his lips, of winning their decision of "yes" to God and his purposes for our needy, greedy, and wounded world.

Have you considered what the Risen Lord, who is with us now, would do if he physically came into our midst? What would he start trying to do that he is not trying to do right now? Isn't he trying to win our hearts, our motives, our attitudes, our dispositions so that they reflect kinship with his Spirit? To win our hearts gives an opportunity for others to see that we are truly sons of the Father. "His Spirit bears testimony with our spirits that we are Sons of God." All this he is doing now!

We affirm the basic message of apocalypse, namely: a steady faith in the unfailing purposes of God, and in his final victory over unrighteousness. Though we can often see and experience the marks of the beast, the beastial claws of cruelty, jealousy, hate, and the lust to dominate those we fear—God's love in us is the only enduring force in our universe. The future belongs to God and his Risen Christ, our Lord. We affirm also the validity of using metaphors in our religious experience, as is done so beautifully in Revelation 4, 5, 19, and 21.

The greatest experience of our lives is the fulfillment of our prayer "Marana tha" (come Lord Jesus). His parousia (presence) does come. We are caught up, not in the sky, but in his purposes, hopes, yearnings, and yes, his prayers for our world. We become friends and coworkers with him here on earth. Immanuel.

SUGGESTIONS FOR GROUP DISCUSSION

1. Ask two persons to report on:
   A. The basic characteristics of apocalyptic literature (see the index of *The Interpreter's Bible;* read the introduction to the commentary on the Book of Revelation in *The Interpreter's Bible*).
   B. Ask a member of the class to diagram on a blackboard or newsprint the two views of our world:
      1) The prescientific view of the Bible—a three-storied universe with a four-square earth floating on water, with sheol (the abode of the dead) under the earth, etc.
      2) The scientific view of earth as seen by our astronauts.

Question: If God is *Spirit,* where is the kingdom of heaven?

Where is the kingdom of heaven? Is it up "there"? How and when does one enter the kingdom of heaven? How does one get close to God—by climbing the highest mountain? How?

2. What do we affirm as we sing "This Is My Father's World"? What do we deny when we sing it? Do you think Satan or God rules our earth? Did Adam give Satan a legal document to possess and rule the earth, as Hal Lindsey says?

3. Ask a panel to discuss the following: (1) God was converted at Calvary by Jesus' death—God now loves those who love him and hates those who hate him; or (2) God, through the life and death of Jesus, reconciled the world unto himself—loving every person, even his enemies.

4. Is the experience of "Immanuel" (God is with us) valid? Or is God far off—up there in a far off heaven?; Does God occasionally come on a cloud from heaven to visit the planet earth?

5. Where is Jesus Christ? What is Jesus Christ the Lord doing now? What motivates him? What are his goals? What methods does he use now to achieve his goals? The day after Jesus died did Jesus Christ change his methods for winning sinners? Can his character and methods of winning converts

be counted on to be the same yesterday, today, and forever?

6. Compare the purposes of the prophet Amos (read chapters 5 and 6) with those of the writer of the book of Daniel. Show how the political, civil, and religious differences between the times of Amos and Daniel made a difference in what and how they taught. Remember that Amos lived in the heyday of Israel (ca. 760 B.C.). Relate the woeful conditions of Daniel's time (168-165 B.C.) under Antiochus Epiphanes and the need for a call to faithfulness and courage.

7. Ask two persons to argue in behalf of one of the two opposing views: (1) the letters to the seven churches were written to the membership of seven churches of Asia Minor by John; or (2) John wrote about the future church—seven periods of church history which cover nineteen hundred years.

8. Discuss the values of the basic message of Revelation:
   A. If it were written in A.D. 95 for persecuted Christians of John's life time;
   B. If Revelation is a foretelling of events two or three (or more) thousands of years in the future.

9. Have you experienced the presence of Christ in your life? What kind of involvement is the Lord seeking from us in order that we be coworkers with him in his purposes now? Does God want us to wait for him to clean up the earth (feed the hungry, seek employment with adequate wages for the oppressed of the earth, lift the heavy burdens that oppress, brutalize, and stunt human life?) Or does God want Christians to be channels of his Spirit wherever there is human need? What is Jesus trying to do now to make the kingdoms of the world become the kingdoms of our Christ?

NOTES

[1] Lindsey, *There's a New World Coming,* p. 91.
[2] *Ibid.,* p. 150; see also Rev. 10:6-7.
[3] *Ibid.,* p. 152.

[4]*Ibid.*, p. 150.

[5]*Ibid.*, p. 186.

[6]*Ibid.*, p. 150.

[7]Cf. Hal Lindsey, *The Late Great Planet Earth* (Grand Rapids, Mich.: Zondervan, 1974), pp. 43, 126.

[8]Lindsey, *Satan Is Alive and Well on Planet Earth,* 48; *There's a New World Coming,* 91.

EXTRATERRESTRIAL LIFE AND INTELLIGENCE
(Christian Faith Can Cope With It)

On July 4, 1976, we the people of the United States (via NASA) will celebrate a great scientific achievement: If all goes well, on that date the first of two unmanned Viking spacecrafts will land on Mars! The second Viking craft will land a short time later.

The purpose of both Viking ships is to seek for possible life on Mars. Scientists in the United States are so convinced of the probability of life on another planet that our government has invested $1,000,000,000 in Project Viking. Each craft contains a life-seeking laboratory.

Each laboratory is a one-foot cube and weighs thirty pounds. Each of the two labs contains 140,000 electronic components (including 122,000 transistors), forty thermostats, three small ovens, bottled radioactive gases, a pocket-sized chromatograph (which can identify the chemical component of the substance the arms of the machine will pick up for study), and a small xenon lamp that will simulate sunshine.[1]

The labs are built to perform three different life-detection experiments. The scientists hope to find some form of life—even if the chemical structures should differ from those on earth! The scientific assumption is that life is not unique to earth, but exists throughout the universe.

THE WHOLE UNIVERSE IS FULL OF GOD'S CREATIVE ACTS

Scientists know that the electromagnetic spectrum is operative throughout the universe. Each of the billions of suns in

Figure 9

The planetary landing spacecraft, Viking, which includes stereo cameras, a weather station, an automated soil analysis laboratory and a biology instrument that can detect life is under assembly at Martin Marietta Aerospace near Denver, Colo. This Viking spacecraft will travel more than 460 million miles from Earth to a soft landing on Mars in 1976 to explore the surface and atmosphere of the planet. Martin Marietta is prime and integrating contractor for the Viking mission to NASA's Langley Research Center, Hampton, Virginia.

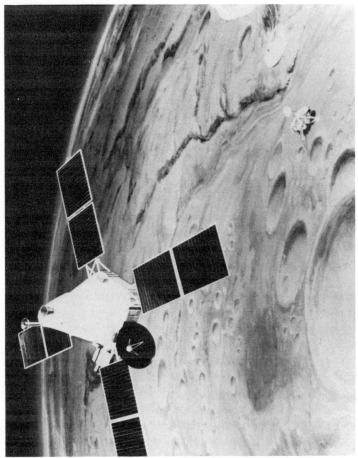

Figure 10   Photo Credit: National Aeronautics and Space Administration

Painting shows unmanned Viking in orbit about Mars with its life-search lander and discarded capsule on the surface of the planet. NASA's first attempt to land instruments on Mars is planned for July 1976 after launch in mid 1975. Four panels supply solar electric power. The white blanket protects the craft's rocket motor from the sun. The circular antenna points to Earth. In addition to the lander's tests for microscopic life both craft will examine the surface and atmosphere with TV cameras and other instruments.

the Milky Way galaxy, as well as in the other billions of galaxies, emits light, x-rays, gamma rays, radio waves, etc. Astronomical spectroscopy has shown that the chemical composition of stars billions of light years away has the same atoms and molecules as in our solar system. Nuclear astrophysics indicates that the same, one hundred-plus, elements (such as hydrogen, nitrogen, oxygen, neon, iron, etc.) found on earth are to be found throughout the universe.[2] God's creation of matter is universal!

Astrochemists report finding molecules necessary for life in interstellar space too. Since 1970 space scientists have found nearly thirty different molecules in interstellar space, including ammonia, water vapor, formaldehyde, carbon monoxide, cyanide, hydrogen cyanide, and cyanoacetylene. Meteorites (from the asteroid belt) contain amino acids. The raw materials which God uses for the development of life (DNA) are in abundance throughout the universe. Physically we are made of star-stuff.

Christian faith can accept the scientist's claim that the DNA would function in a universe of billions of stars and planets in the same way it does in our solar system. For God designed the DNA, with its 64 words, as the *universal* language of life. The genetic code is universal. All living things, on earth and in the heavens, are related in ways we never dreamed of previously. We affirm: All things come from thee, O God.

INTELLIGENT LIFE THROUGHOUT THE UNIVERSE?

Persons may readily admit that the physical universe (of light, matter, life) was, and is being, created by God—but what about creatures in his image? What about the creation of spiritual beings—are they limited to life on earth only, or is it possible that God has fathered spiritual (intelligent, moral, aesthetic, religious) beings on other planets of his universe?

Are there any scientists who consider intelligent life possible on other planets? The answer is affirmative. Dr. Frank Drake (now at Cornell University) was one of the first to make a systematic attempt to devise a method of communicating with extraterrestrial life. Dr. Drake organized Project Ozma in 1960. Using the eighty-five foot radiotelescope of the National Radio Astronomy Observatory at Green Bank, West Virginia, Dr. Drake and other scientists listened on the 21 cm natural hydrogen line for 400 hours (two weeks) to the stars. The two stars were Epsilon-Eridani and Tau-Ceti. Though nothing was heard, it was the beginning of many serious discussions concerning the method earthlings should use in their attempt to communicate with beings in outer space.

Scientists at Green Bank National Radio Astronomy Observatory and at the Gorky Radiophysical Institute in the Soviet Union are continuing research in the field of interterrestrial communication.

The international scientific community has shown considerable interest. In 1971 a conference was held in Soviet Armenia, sponsored by the Soviet Academy of Sciences and the National Academy of Sciences of the United States. The chairman of the delegation from the United States was Carl Sagan, who has described that conference in his book, *Cosmic Connection*. Dr. Sagan writes that the delegates to the conference were drawn from the professions of mathematics, astronomy, physics, biology, electronics, computer technology, cryptography, chemistry, anthropology, history, and archaeology. The conclusion of the conference was that "the chances of there being extraterrestrial communicative societies and our present technological ability to contact them were both sufficiently high that a serious search was warranted."[3]

It is significant that there are serious scientists who think governments on earth should plan and work together in attempts to communicate with interterrestrial intelligence.

I am convinced God did not create the universe, with its

millions of galaxies, so that *only* mankind on the small planet earth could have fellowship with him. The great, purposive, loving, and omniscient God must have desired and purposed to have intelligent beings on other planets too. The educated guess of radio-astronomers and astrochemists, as we have noted, is that there is intelligent life on other planets besides that of earth. I accept this hypothesis as valid.

If God created intelligent life on other planets, Genesis 1 might be expanded to read: God created not only mankind, but also intelligent beings in his universe. And he created them by using the three energy systems: the electromagnetic spectrum, matter, DNA. To these God added the dimension we call spirituality. We may properly ask if intelligent beings other than human beings respond to God. Do they respond better than those on the planet earth? Are they more intelligent, more moral, more aesthetic, in better (more effective) relationship to God than we? Or are they less intelligent, less moral, less aesthetic, less faithful in their commitment to God? The answer must include the probability of intelligent life on various planets being on different levels of achievement. Some planets may have highly developed intellectual life, others lower than on earth.

Let us consider some implications for Christians if God has made intelligent beings throughout his universe.

THE NATURE OF SPIRITUAL BEINGS CREATED IN THE IMAGE OF GOD

The answer to the question "What is the nature of spiritual beings created in the image of God?" is determined by the nature of God. And, strangely, what Christians consider to be the nature of God varies considerably even among Christians. For example, which predominates justice or love? There are those who rule out God in their thinking about the nature of mankind. Erich Von Däniken rules out God in his books

Chariots of the Gods? and *Gods from Outer Space.* Let me illustrate this anti-God movement in Von Däniken's unscientific, nonbiblical, nontheological, and totally nonarchaeological perspective.

Erich Von Däniken apparently knows little or no Hebrew, so he abuses the word for God in Genesis 1. Genesis 1:1 reads: In the beginning God (Elohim) created; Genesis 1:26 states that God (Elohim) said: let us make man in our image. But for the beautiful Hebrew word Elohim (which is the plural form for majesty of the one God whom Moses later acknowledged to be one being and whom he then called Yahweh) Von Däniken substitutes the words: creatures from outer space.

So everytime Von Däniken uses the word "gods" he does not mean God, but intelligent beings (creatures) from outer space. These creatures came to earth millenia ago, he claims; and they artificially impregnated some female primates and thus created earth's first intelligent beings called man, homo sapiens. Millenia later the space beings returned and found that their experiment had failed, so they tried again. This time Von Däniken states that some of their own DNA had been programmed for knowledge of smelting copper, language, writing, morality, and religion; and they developed a mutation called Sumerians. Thus came the Sumerians of 3500 B.C. to the Tigris-Euphrates Valley! So fictionizes Erich Von Däniken.

Von Däniken violates accepted discoveries of Near East archaeology and modern biblical studies. He writes that it was not God who appeared to Ezekiel on the Chebar Canal—rather the creatures from outer space. These creatures from outer space, Von Däniken claims, also designed the Ark of the Covenant. We have to ask, did they come ca. 10,000 B.C., then 3,500 B.C., then in 1250 B.C., then 586 B.C.? The Ark was electrically charged, he says, with several hundred volts. The border and golden crown served to charge a condenser which was formed by the golden plates and a positive and negative conductor. If in addition, writes Von Däniken, one of the two cherubim on the mercy seat acted as a magnet, then the loudspeaker—a communication system between Moses and the spaceship—was perfect. Von Däniken should not have written the next sentence, for it reveals his total and abysmal ignorance of the Mosaic Ark. He writes that without consulting the book of Exodus, he seems to remember that the Ark was often surrounded by flashing sparks and that Moses made use of this "transmitter" whenever he needed help and advice.[4]

Von Däniken's references to the Bible are sheer nonsense. Yet so many people are excited by his tremendous imagination and by the exciting films of what appear to be ancient airstrips on Easter Island and in Peru, that they all too quickly adopt everything he says. One should learn to weed out the considerable amount of exegetical trash to enjoy his book. Perhaps I should also add that Von Däniken knows less about biblical archaeology than he does about the Bible, as shown in his treatment of Ezekiel's experience of God on the Chebar Canal as an experience with a space man in a helicopter.

Let us return now to the biblical account in Genesis 1:26, which states that God created man in his image. What does it mean to be created in the image of God? We should recall that it cannot mean anything physical, for God is Spirit. God has no hair, no physical eyes, no feet, no hands, no physical body, so he does not literally sit on a physical throne surrounded with physical beings.

To be created in the image of God means that a creature shares some of the spiritual potentialities which are in the divine Spirit, God. We have postulated that there is life on other planets—probably thousands or millions of planets. We now ask if some of these living creatures are intelligent. Can they distinguish between what is true and what is false? Are they able to choose between what is ethically right or wrong? Do they experience moral choice? Do they have eyes and possibly color cones so that they can experience beautifully colored objects? Can they differentiate between what is ugly and what is beautiful? Can they relate to their Creator? Do they experience a relationship which gives them a sense of awe and wonder as expressed by an Einstein or a psalmist? Do they exhibit human qualities? Do they share a sense of loyalty, honor, justice, mercy, kindness, selfishness, or cooperativeness? How intelligent are they?

HOW WOULD WE COMMUNICATE WITH SPACE-BEINGS?

I recall reading in the *Saturday Review* (January 2, 1960, p. 39 ff) that the National Radio-Astronomy Observatory at Green Bank, West Virginia, was seeking to detect and record radio signals that might be emitted from other planets in the Milky Way; and they were preparing to send signals into outer space in the hope that intelligent beings would receive and respond to their message.

Dr. Frank Drake and Dr. Bernard Oliver worked out a code which could be sent from Green Bank to outer space. It was a message that uses 1,271 ones and zeros—the binary system of two prime numbers which is used in computer terminology. Programmers of computers call them "bits." So there were 1,271 bits which could be sent out from Green Bank to outer space.

It was assumed that those (in outer space) who received these 1,271 bits will be mathematically minded. These intelligent minds would immediately recognize the fact that this number (1,271) is the product of two numbers: 41 x 31. This would suggest a message written within either 41 lines of 31 bits each or 31 lines of 41 bits each. The bits, we recall are like the numbers 0 and 1. The 0's would act as blank spaces. When thirty-one lines are filled with the forty-one bits a picture is immediately recognized. The message is quite clear: the planet (earth) transmitting the message is inhabited by mammals who are two-legged bisexual creatures, whose offspring are a third to a half their size.

A scale on the far right of the picture is labeled in a binary code and shows the approximate height of the mammals (man) to be eleven units high—twenty-one centimeters (about seven and one-half feet) tall. Of course earthlings are not 7½′ tall, but this is as close to the height of man as Dr. Oliver could get within the limits of available space. Symbols across the top indicate our basic elements: hydrogen, carbon, oxygen—which suggests the chemical basis of life on earth. The male creature points to the left side of the picture to the third planet from the sun (indicated in the upper left corner of the picture)—suggesting we are the third planet from the sun. Waves of water are seen, with a fish swimming in it.[5]

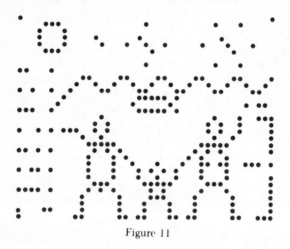

Figure 11

NASA'S HOPES TO COMMUNICATE

In very recent years NASA has been exploring our solar system through Pioneers 10 and 11. These spacecraft represent our first probes from our own planetary system. Pioneers 10 and 11 journeyed to Jupiter, sending back messages to astronomers with much new information. The two small spacecrafts (Pioneers 10 and 11) are continuing on beyond Jupiter, representing our first probe into the vastness of interstellar space. The Pioneer spacecraft carries a pictorial plaque.

It is designed to show scientifically educated inhabitants of some other star system—who might intercept it millions of years from now—when Pioneer was launched, from where, and by what kind of beings. The design is etched into a gold-anodized aluminum plate, 152 by 229 millimeters (6 by 9 inches), attached to the spacecraft's antenna support struts in a position to help shield it from erosion by interstellar dust. The radiating lines at left represent the positions of 14 pulsars—cosmic sources of radio energy—arranged to indicate our Sun as the home star of the launching civilization. The "1-" symbols at the ends of the lines are binary numbers that represent the frequencies of these pulsars at the time of launch of Pioneer 10 relative to that of the hydrogen atom shown at the upper left with a "1" unity symbol. The hydrogen atom is thus used as a "universal clock," and the regular decrease in the frequencies of the pulsars will enable another civilization to determine the time that has elapsed since Pioneer 10 was launched. The hydrogen atom is also used as a "universal yardstick" for sizing the human figures and outline of the spacecraft shown on the right. The hydrogen wavelength—about 8 inches—multiplied by the binary number representing "8" shown next to the woman gives her height—64 inches. The figures represent the type of creature that created Pioneer. The man's hand is raised in a gesture of good will. Across the bottom are the planets, ranging outward from the Sun, with the spacecraft's trajectory arching away from Earth, passing Mars, and swinging by Jupiter.[6] (See figure 12.)

Again, I want to make the point that there are many learned scientists who not only accept the concept of intelligent beings in extraterrestrial space, but are betting their lives through dedicated years of work to start the process of communication between human beings of earth and intelligent beings of outer space. Project Viking (see the introduction to this chapter) also presupposes such scientific expectation of extraterrestrial intelligence.

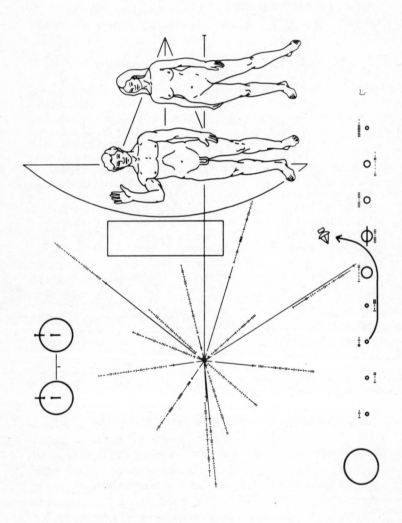

Figure 12

We started out by asking if there was any intelligence in outer space. We have answered the question in part by stating that at least many persons high in our government and in radio-astronomy of the USA certainly believe so. I personally find this a most fascinating probability and hope that such a probe will bring communication between intelligent beings separated by billions of miles and many light years. I might add that I also find the reverse to be fascinating: to consider it possible that communication can take place by intelligent beings visiting our earth seeking to communicate with us. However we have too little information about UFOs to draw an affirmative conclusion.

SUPPOSE GOD HAS CREATED INTELLIGENT BEINGS THROUGHOUT THE UNIVERSE

What a thrill it would be if we were to receive a response from outer space at Green Bank, West Virginia, or at the National Astronomy and Ionosphere Center run by Cornell University in Arecibo, Puerto Rico. Probably it would be a simple pictograph. However, it could be (if they were more intelligent than we) that they could include in their message to us a simple scheme for us to develop a more adequate communication mechanism. One possibility comes to my mind: why not develop an alphabet based on the atomic numbers of the various elements of our universe? Hydrogen has one electron, let that be the letter A, etc.

Assuming a response, if we sent a message, we would obviously know that highly developed intelligent beings exist. We would then want to know what they looked like, what their molecular structure is, which element predominates; whether they experience morality, beauty, and religion(s). The fact of a message from outer space would imply that the senders of the message were not only mathematicians, but also had a well developed language. For you cannot develop mathematics to a high degree without the ability to think abstractly and of concrete needs and applications. So language (the ability to read, write, and communicate) would be an inevitable corollary of their intelligence.

But would they be able to experience morality? Would they have the ability to make moral choices? Did God build into these creatures from another planet a sense of law (national, global, interglobal) through which they have found that intelligent creatures get along better, if not best? What would these kinds of principles, laws, or regulations be like?

The Dr. Fred Hoyle, undoubtedly one of the greatest astronomers of all times, accepted the probability of intelligent beings throughout the universe. In fact, in 1964 he was thinking in terms of a galactic library. Dr. Hoyle speculated that there was an interchange of messages going on in the Milky Way galaxy on a vast scale all the time. And that persons on the planet earth were as unaware of this communication network as are pygmies in the Australian forests who are unaware of the radio and television messages that flash at the speed of light around the earth. Dr. Fred Hoyle offered an educated guess that there might be a million or more subscribers to a great galactic directory (like a telephone directory) which carries the name, number, and dial code for intelligent beings in the Milky Way.[7] Keep in mind that Dr. Fred Hoyle was serious, he was not joking!

Dr. Hoyle pointed out that an exchange of messages with the nearest inhabited planet could take a few centuries. But even such slow communication would be worthwhile, he argued. The messages would carry the big ideas, not the daily baseball scores, from one planet to another. Dr. Hoyle suggested that an interchange of ideas on where the dangers lie in interpersonal and interglobal relations would be of inestimable value. A computer used in a galactic library of the Milky Way would gather and store the information on which policies lead to atomic/thermonuclear war and which policies

avoid such global catastrophies. Such information might lead
to the most revolutionary step in human thinking.

Dr. Hoyle paraphrased one of our beautiful psalms when he
expressed his confidence in a galactic library by saying, "I will
lift up mine eyes to the sky from which cometh my help." He
just might have some truth here. What do you think? Incidentally, how great is your God? Is he super galactic? Or is he only
the God of earth as Benjamin Franklin thought? Are there
other, greater gods? Is there only one God of the universe? Is
he the Creator of the 250 billion stars in our galaxy, the Milky
Way? Is he Creator of the billions of galaxies? Is this my
Father's universe? Can I hear him "speak" everywhere?

A half-dozen years before Dr. Fred Hoyle stirred up some of
our firm beliefs, Methodist Bishop Bromley Oxnam stretched
my imagination to an even greater degree.

THE FIRST INTERPLANETARY CONFERENCE ON FAITH

In "The Invisible Fire" Bishop Oxnam responded to a question
which had been asked a dozen great minds: What do you
think will be the greatest event of the decade (1960s) ahead?
He declared that in the decade ahead the most dramatic event
would be an interplanetary conference on religious faith. The
conference would be attended by the finest minds of the
planets—perhaps those in our galaxy, the Milky Way? The
conference, if it had but one delegate from each planet, would
be so large that all the houses in New York City could not
house the delegates! Bishop Oxnam suggested that the conference would be made possible because of the scientific mastery of space travel.

Of course that conference was not held. But the thought has
prodded my mind for over a decade and a half. I would like to
describe a make-believe interplanetary conference on religious faith. Put on your hat used for imagination, close your

eyes, and let's be visionary—not of the heavenly assize, but one that might approach it "in the heavens," that is, somewhere on a planet in outer space.

First, the purpose of the interplanetary conference on religious faith would be for the various delegates to share the best concepts of the religions of all the planets and to state the revelations of God to the various intelligent beings present. Of course the sessions would be televised for all interplanetary beings to hear and see. Obviously, the first requirement would be a principle of theological pluralism: a tolerance based on a desire to understand the other creatures' experiences with God. Dogmatism would have no place among them, for the primary principle which called them together was the principle of love, respect, and acceptance of each and all by all.

The question to be raised at the first interplanetary conference on religious faith would deal with their perceptions of the nature, purpose, and activities of God, and their relationship to God as experienced by the delegates. How did God make himself known to the inhabitants of Orion, of Earth, of Epsilon-Etidan? Perhaps, by the infinite stretching of our imagination, some delegates had anticipated such a meeting several light years earlier and arrived at the right planet at the right time for the sessions.

Before you consider such an interplanetary meeting of our own galaxy to be impossible, consider the following:

Einstein, in his theory of special (as distinguished from general) relativity, discussed the effects of travel at very great speeds approaching the speed of light. An object "shrinks" as it moves faster, and time dilates. A spacecraft, approaching the speed of light, would be much reduced in size. (Only rays of light travel at 186,282 miles per second!) Occupants of a spacecraft approaching the speed of light could travel many thousands of light years during their physical lifetime (of say seventy years). Einstein's theory of time dilation is considered a fact: time dilation is measurable!

Suppose as some astrophysicists assume, intelligent life may be 1,000 or 10,000 or maybe a million years ahead of earthlings' culture (and knowledge). They would work with laws of nuclear physics and of time not yet formalized into formulas by earthlings. Dr. Carl Sagan, states that it is entirely possible for space travel of the future to move at such great speed that a person(s) could traverse our galaxy—with a diameter of about sixty-thousand light years—and return to the earth in less than a human lifetime! Of course a return to the starting point (in that human lifetime) would be to an earth sixty thousand light years ahead of the time of departure (so all friends would have died long ago). Dr. Sagan concluded that "time travel into the future is thus not an immediate prospect, but it is a prospect conceivable for an advanced technology on planets of other stars."[8]

If close-to-the-speed-of-light space travel is conceivable by the laws of nuclear physics by more advanced civilizations on God-made planets of other stars—then, does our proposed Interplanetary Conference on Religion stretch our imaginations unduly?

Also, we must admit, from the above logic, the high possibility of visitations to earth by some of God's "space-creatures" from other planets. UFOs are a possibility, in terms of Einstein's special relativity, concerning the shrinkage of very fast moving vehicles (from changes being made in the nuclear particles) and time dilation.

Well, let your imagination run free. You are viewing the great interplanetary conference hall. Around a huge elliptical, mahogany-like table, backed up by elliptical rows of chairs for three representatives from each of the planets, the delegates gathered—each wondering what protocol required for seating arrangements.

A great electronic organ broke the silence with its unearthly (interstellar) sounds; some *earthly* delegate was heard to remark: "It must be the Pythagorean 'Music of the Spheres.'"

The frequencies of the music were such that each delegate heard in his own tongue that the Holy Creator and Father of all was present and that each should be seated (or stand or be at rest as the case required) at a place at the table closest to them. Protocol did not include noting which delegate came from the farthest, nearest, richest, densest, greenest, reddest, shortest- or longest-hour per day, or the oldest planet from the newest constellation, nor the newest planet from the oldest constellation. Delegates assumed an equality which they accepted as coming from the Creator and Father.

Another movement on the interplanetary electronics organ, sounded by a Wagnerian-like organist (whose playing was obviously tempered somewhat by Bachian fugues), called the first session of the interplanetary conference on religion to order. Again, for those whose receptors were geared to high frequencies and to those who heard only tones of lowest frequencies, the vibrations were so orchestrated as to communicate in hundreds of interstellar languages.

The committee who planned the meetings had planned well. Placed near each delegate was either a telescopic or microscopic device so that he could see the delegates at their various places at the gigantic table. But more interesting than that were the conditions, you might say the prerequisites, for attending the session. Some creatures came from planet Earth, which fact required them to be encased in space-suit-like equipment so that they could deal adequately with the cold temperature, the low pressure, and the lack of oxygen which had to be supplied artificially. Another delegate, whose basic molecular structure, NH_3 (ammonia), was similar to that of the earthlings (whose basic molecular structure was water, H_2O), had to have a special space-like suit with connecting tubes for essential ammonia. The delegates were in transparent "housing" equipment so their physical responses and attitudes could be seen by all delegates.

While the delegates seated themselves around the gigantic

table, there was an audible hum of many noises as the delegates responded to their view of the various shapes, colors, smells, and appendages which their codelegates exhibited. Of course the delegates had known of such diversity of sizes, shapes, and in some cases different molecular bases for their physical beings. But though they had known cognitively of these differences, it was admittedly quite an emotional experience to be seated next to intelligent beings whose size, shape, and appearance could not have been conceived with their imagination. It took a long time for the delegates to get a good "sense" of each other with their varying sensors. (For example, some eyes could read only by use of infrared light; others by black light; while earthlings used the spectrum of light; some had biotic eyes that scanned large areas quickly—a 6' x 4' plaque was read in three seconds; other eyes were adjusted to the microscopic so they had to use specially prepared lenses to read the meaning of printed messages on the 6' x 4' plaque.) The methods of greetings and recognition by the delegates would make a story in itself. Some nodded their head, others moved a large left ear, some blinked twice, one tapped his third hand softly on the table top, another sniffed three times emitting a low pitch. And there was only friendliness, no hostility present.

The newly created interstellar electronic organ pealed out a magnificent prelude. The beat was so ingeniously devised that each delegate heard a message in his own way. The call to worship had been clearly heard by all. The first interplanetary conference on religion opened its session with a worship service. One of the unforgettable features was the opening litany in which all delegates participated. Part of that litany and the new media communications presentations are noted as follows: (We should note that all verbal expressions and even some nonverbal, were simultaneously translated into the medium used by each delegate.)

LEADER: *In the beginning God said: Let there be light.*

(And immediately an expression of light was observed by all: through hundreds of tiny holes in the ceiling tiny prisms spread the spectrum of light across the entire group. Each delegate experienced the colors of the rainbow as it caressed his person. The delegates responded with an obvious awareness of a phrase similar to that of the earthling Ezekiel (1:28): There was a rainbow around and in back of the Throne of God. And that rainbow had touched each of their lives with promise.)

DELEGATES: *God is light. We offer to Thee, light of our life, our expressions of appreciation for your creation of light, its rainbow promises of peace, and for the infinite uses of light.*

LEADER: *For creating the energy system of your electromagnetic spectrum. . . .*

(For five—or could it have been twenty-five—minutes the delegates observed various New Media presentations of the uses of radiation of energy: radio waves, television waves, x-rays, radar, sonar systems, microwaves, macrowaves (used for baking and cooking for heat on thousands of planets), the use of light in photosynthesis—for growth of plants, trees, vegetables, animals and persons, etc.)

DELEGATES: *We bow in reverence and awe at thy creative and providential genius, O Father and Creator of all.*

LEADER: *For having created receptors with which to see, to feel, to recognize, to comprehend objects and colors, and to permit each delegate here assembled to know one another.*

DELEGATES: (As they looked at one another.) *We thank thee, our Father, for having made us physically in varieties of colors, shapes, sizes, and with varying appendages. For biological plurality we give thee thanks.*

LEADER: *We thank thee for creating the energy system of matter, for out of thine own being thou has brought energy from which all things come.*

(For a moment the room was darkened, and then there was a period of time for silent worship and adoration as the new media uniquely displayed the structure of atoms. One by one unique chandeliers began to be slowly illuminated—each in accordance to a plan. For each chandelier—over a hundred of them—contained a number of lights according to the number of electrons of that element. Thus the first lovely chandelier had one light since hydrogen has but one electron. The oxygen chandelier had eight lights; the uranium chandelier had 238 lights in its beautiful design. An interesting feature of the chandeliers was that the lights in each "atomic" chandelier were at varying distances from their centers according to the distance of the electrons from their nuclei. For example: the nucleus of an atom of Uranium 238 has 92 electrons, so the

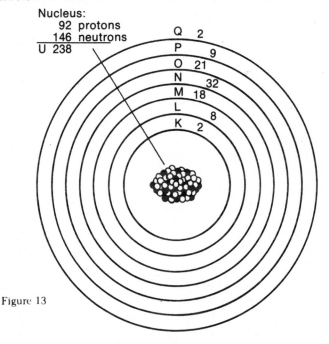

Figure 13

Uranium atom has 92 electrons; 7 shells

lights were arranged in seven spherical shells around the nucleus: the inner shell K had 2 lights; the second shell L had 8; the next shell M, 18; shell N had 32; O had 21; P had 9; Q had 2.)

DELEGATES: We praise thee for thy wonderful creation of matter—created from thy energizing will to the energy from which all atoms come—and for the brilliant system by which atoms are bonded together to form molecules and compounds.

LEADER: For thy creative Word which superimposed the sixty-four basic words upon inorganic matter by which we have life.

(Then there is another interval of time during which a display of the DNA, the double helix, was presented before them in three dimensional form via laser beam and halography. In quick, but clear and precise sequence, the double helix was presented, showing the use of the four basic letters (A, C, T, G) in forming the two-letter rungs of the ladder of the DNA; then showing how the ends of the rungs (the verticals of the ladder) were so intricately connected to a sugar molecule and that in turn to a phosphate—thus forming one of the three letter words (codon) of the DNA. Then a demonstration of the DNA splitting lengthwise; and its reformation into a new DNA, and the concurrent movement of $_m$RNA into the cytoplasm where it produced protein, which made the correct choice of amino acids, carefully choosing one at a time from a possible twenty amino acids those which were absolutely required. Then the new media demonstrated the way hereditary traits via genes and chromosomes were reproduced and became a part of the DNA—so that every molecule in each of the delegates' bodies contained the same coded information for their physical growth and development. What a glorious hour of worship as the creative acts of God unfolded so vividly before their very eyes.)

DELEGATES: Blessings, glory, wisdom, and thanks for thy providential creation and maintenance of thy law and crea-

tive Word in continuing to create new forms in our days.

LEADER: For thy loving care that created by thy processes from simple to ever more complex forms living creatures made in your image.

DELEGATES: We are grateful, Father, for the gift of spiritual life, for the ability to choose between right and wrong, to differentiate between the beautiful and the ugly, to choose between the false and the true, to know that thou who has created us seeks our fellowship, our love, and personal relationship with each of us. We bless thee, we thank thee.

(Then a brief interlude during which three-dimensional symbols seemed to move suspended above the delegates' tables, at first without meaning to most delegates, but then all delegates began to understand as they recognized symbols from their own backgrounds: the cross on which Jesus was crucified; a rack on which another person in whom the Word has become incarnate on their planet had been stretched till he died: instruments of torture, including drugs which had sought to permanently change the attitudes and commitments of those being tortured. After a lengthy silence, "time, two times and half a time," the litany concluded with a prayer of gratitude.)

LEADERS AND DELEGATES: (And they prayed—each in his own tongue, according to his varied frequencies, and in various physical stances, the prayer each had been taught on his planet by him who had suffered in their behalf—the Lord's Prayer. The Apostle Paul, writing in Colossians was right: Jesus Christ was and is the Christ of the universe, and Christ's prayer has been heard and learned throughout the universe. God's fullest revelation has been made throughout his universe. The Word has become flesh and lived among spiritual beings throughout the universe.)

What a glorious and unique hour of worship as the mighty acts of God's creation unfolded dramatically before their eyes. The concluding moments were a sense of affirmation that

Jesus Christ, the Lord of the universe, had stood in their midst in his risen power.

All of which opened up the discussions for the interplanetary conference. They had all studied at their "universities" about the various energy systems by which God had formed their planets: light, matter, DNA, and the new life of the Spirit. They spoke of their scientific knowledge and of their faith, and it was immediately understood by others in their own tongue! It was a type of Pentecostal experience, and each and all felt the presence and empowerment of the Holy Spirit upon them.

But all was not perfection. The delegates, as we observed, were of different sizes, shapes, colors, and even smells. Some delegates were only eight inches tall and had arrived in small spheres—but the spheres had tremendous mobility and could expand a protective facade that made their space craft look one hundred times larger than it really was. An interesting event happened with the representative of earth who sat near the eight-inch tall creature they dubbed Tom Thumb.

On the second morning of sessions, Tom Thumb sat at his appointed place near the three representatives of earth. Though great discussions were reverberating across the hallway, Tom sat absolutely motionless—with one exception: a barely noticeable movement of his tiny finger every three or four seconds. Suddenly the chairman called for a response from Tom Thumb as representative of his planet. He did not hear his name called for he was deeply absorbed in meditation. One of the trio from earth gently nudged his tall chair on which he was seated. He apologized and said: "This morning I found a huge—two inch by two inch—poster-like placard on my desk. On careful scrutiny I quickly discovered that it contained 848 pages called the Old and New Testament." Tom Thumb had accidentally found a library "fish" that had fallen from the black daily calendar of an earth delegate adjacent to him. The 2″ x 3″ card (the "fish") was a copy of the entire Bible. The card was microfilmed, so that it was a series of dots, and wherever spots appeared, each "spot" was actually fifteen pages microfilmed from a large family Bible of 848 pages!

Obviously, Tom's biotic eyes were accustomed to reading microfilm with his natural vision, so he was excited by what he read. He said in his deep voice: "I have read: 'The heavens declare the Glory of God and the firmament showeth his handiwork'; also, 'The Word of our God endureth forever.' I read in what is called John 1:1 'In the beginning was the Word, and the Word was God, and without the Word was not anything made that was made. . . .' I was so engrossed and in such hearty agreement that I failed to listen to the discussion." (Of course the earth delegates had been unaware that he was reading from their Bible—which Tom had cut into fifty-five invisible pages of microfilm reading matter.) The delegates applauded, each in his own way. They applauded, for unwittingly he had answered the question being discussed: Who has formed the universe? Does he continue to live? From what source did living things come into being? Our Bible answered these questions!

Then it was that an unseen chorus joined the electronic organ with a Hallelujah Chorus that sounded strangely familiar to the trio from earth, and apparently so to the other delegates too!

GOD'S CONCERN FOR FREEDOM

Not only those who represented the Judeo-Christian experience of earth, but also those from other planets witnessed to the faith-claim that the supreme being, God, revealed himself in his saving acts in behalf of his creatures. As Moses had experienced God's redemptive acts in setting his people free from oppression in Egypt, so others witnessed to similar saving acts on their planets. God, the Savior/Redeemer, was interested in the poor, the oppressed, the imprisoned, the blind—those whose God-like attributes (of mind, emotion, will, and purposes) were denied the possibility of achieving their self-fulfillment because of imposed and coerced limitations by others.

The delegates witnessed to similar experiences that history (on their planets) was the arena of God's activity. God's activity, they said, is often recognized in the struggles of those, like Israel in Egypt, who strive for freedom from oppression; and in the divine initiative in leading them to a promised land where oppression ceases and peace comes as the fruit of justice and love. One delegate paraphrased Isaiah by saying: "All history is full of the glory of God."

THE UNIQUENESS OF FAITH

The communication network at the conference was so planned that microphones picked up all remarks—even the side remarks of delegates. One side remark, not intended for all, yet carried to the electronic receivers of all delegates was a whispered statement to a fellow delegate: "God is different for us. Our great father of the faith, who was guided by God to save our people from oppression of a neighboring planet taught us to say: 'Is it not in thy going with us, so that we are distinct, I and thy people, from all other people that are upon the face of the planet?' And God answered: 'Yes, Immanuel, I am and will be with you!'"

But no sooner was the statement made, than countless delegates overhearing the side remark nodded affirmatively and said, "Amen, that is our experience too." The delegate from earth said: "We have a similar statement in fact, word for word, in our sacred book called Exodus, chapter 33:14. How similar God's promises and actions are to all those of every nation and planet who call upon him. For in calling upon him they discover that he is near."

GOD SEEKS COVENANT RELATIONSHIPS

This sense of Immanuel (God is with us) led to a discussion of another attribute of God which grew out of the deeds/acts of God: God, they proclaimed, is a covenant-seeking God. God seeks personal relationships with individuals, with small groups of individuals, and with the entire planet; now God seeks covenant relationships with planets. A new understanding of God was affirmed: God is the God of all creatures in the universe who seek him and his will for all other creatures.

One of the delegates from the constellation of Pisces remarked: "God seems to have revealed himself, not through verbal proclamations, propositions, and statements, but through his saving acts and relationships with his creatures. Implications concerning the nature and character of God—such as his love, justice, judgment, concern, good will—are deduced from the divine actions of the Lord God." The conference agreed that this was a common experience of creatures from all the planets. The verbal agreement, magnified by electronic devices (even though incredibly small since molecules were used for the miniaturized circuitry) created a terrific cacophony of noises. One delegate's whisper reached them all: "Make a joyful noise unto the Lord."

The closing session dealt with a single faith claim: Delegates from each of the planets witnessed that there was always one single outstanding "creature" whose life seemed to be a full expression of what previous persons who at their best thinking had thought about God. Of course they had different words for him, even as the earthlings had some seventy titles for him, such as the Only One, the Begotten One, the Elect One, the Son, the Son of God—though their favorite titles were: the Messiah, Christ, and Son of God.

It was recognized that God had incarnated himself in a unique way in the life of one person on each of the planets. Tom Thumb had read with his microscopic eyes in the microscopic Bible of the earth delegate just the right words: "In the beginning was the Word. . . . In him was life, and the life was the light of men. . . . The true light that enlightens every man [spiritual being] was coming into the world [universe]. He was in the world [the universe], and the world was made through him, yet the world knew him not. . . . And the Word became flesh and dwelt among us, full of grace and truth; we have beheld his glory, glory as of the only Son from the Father" (John 1:1-14).

Strange looking delegates, with the most peculiar facial and bodily habits, witnessed to the way the universal Christ had come to them. Many witnessed to their refusal to accept him until his unwarranted death proved his divine love—a love that made him lay down his life for others that they might find the Father of us all, experience forgiveness of sin, and commit themselves to his motives, purposes, and intents toward his spirit creatures. Each and all bore witness to the life-giving love of the eternal and universal logos (the Word). He was indeed as silent as a lamb at his slaughter at a temple—he opened not his mouth in cursing or condemnation. Rather he prayed for them and asked forgiveness for their dogmatically closed minds. Because he died in pain, yet with such compassion, and love, they soon saw something not seen before: they saw the glory of God reflected in the face of their Redeemer and Savior. He had revealed God's depth of love.

As a body they rose as an anthem rang out: "Worthy is the lamb that was slain," followed by a great chorus singing Hallelujah. "The kingdoms of our planets shall become the kingdoms of our universal Christ."

SUPPOSE AN EXTRATERRESTRIAL CREATURE CALLED ON YOU

Suppose you encountered a creature the like of which you had never heard nor seen. How would you respond? Can you think theologically about creatures that differ radically from you? We need to ask ourselves again: What does it mean to be created in the image of God? Does being in the image of God require us to have a certain number of fingers or toes? Hair of a certain texture—preferably like mine? Does being in the image of God require eyes to be of the same shape as mine? What does a creature have to look like to be a son or daughter of God? The interplanetary conference of religious faith discovered that size, shape, color, texture, and weight had nothing to do with those characteristics which define a person as being in the image of God.

As a matter of fact, the conference characterized those creatures who are not in the image of God as those whose attitudes, motives, and purposes are not at one with those of their common Father. Being a child of God, the conference affirmed, is not a matter of certain physical characteristics, but of spiritual qualities. True, all creatures of the universe have a common heritage in the basic sixty-four letters of the DNA molecule. Yet, similar physical structures don't make a spiritual kinship. True kinship is found in mutual at-onement of attitudes, hopes, purposes, ideals. And that great at-onement is found in the style of life and teachings of the Christ the Lord of the universe and in the continuity of his life as Risen Lord who is with us creatures always—no matter where we are.

Recently at a Bible conference in the South I was asked what I would say to a nine-year-old boy who had been talking to two fishermen who claimed they had been taken aboard an unidentified spacecraft. The boy had heard the younger of the men say he had been so scared he fainted. The older man stated that he had seen strangely shaped intelligent creatures, with a blue light about them, who took him gently but by force into their spacecraft—though none of them ever hurt him. The mother asked: "What should I tell my nine-year-old son, who as evening approaches, carries a small quilt everywhere he goes for fear he may see one of these creatures, and if he does see one he can hide under his quilt?"

I told the woman that the apostle Paul wrote in Colossians that Jesus Christ is the *Christ* (the Word) of the universe (Colossians 1:15-20). Paul was stating that Christ is not only Christ of earth, but of the whole universe. Christ taught by many parables and other teachings that God is a loving God. If God created the universe, then he created the universe as a loving God would create it. If God created intelligent beings on other planets, which I assume he did, then these intelligent creatures are in the image of God too. They have the capacity for truth, goodness, beauty, and faith. Let's trust God's creative acts—wherever, whatever, and whenever they come. Let us teach our children to trust all God's creatures who are endowed with abilities for intelligence, aesthetics, truth, and faith—especially those who are engaged in the disciplines of life-fulfillment.

I was thinking the other day what I would do if some extraterrestrial intelligent creature of God's designing and creation should show up at my house and ask me to show him a number of things about Nashville. For example, What is a family? Where would I take him to show him what a Christian family is really like. (Where would you take him?) Or where would I take him to illustrate what church school classes are doing for ministering to the needs of persons. I wondered where I would take him to share experiences of our community of faith at worship. I thought of my local church. Then I wondered about this large-headed, purple-colored creature with vertical eyes, two long arms (no feet) by which he propelled his body—suppose I took him to church. We would "walk" down the transept, move up the nave to the third seat and enter our regular pew. What would be the reaction of those around me as we bowed for prayer?

The question is all too touchy: Does a creature who is worthy of worshiping with me or studying the Word with me have to look like me? Must he have the same kind of appendages (feet and hands) and skin. Suppose he had two antennas on his head and wore a small cap over each antenna. Possibly he crossed his antennae when he prayed; and honored God by putting a drop of one of the basic elements in the creation of all living things—formaldehyde—on each tip of his two antennas? The question is: Can I pray amidst a stench? Must I smell the perfume of flowers to pray at my best? Well, lots of questions begin to arise, don't they? But the real question for us and for any creature from outer space who might call on me (us) is: Are we made in the image of God? And do we so live that we reflect God's attitudes toward all he created? Do we feel God's empathy for those to whom injustice, hunger, loneliness, and pain has come? When jealousy, greed, and hate arise, do we weep with the Risen Lord because "they knew not the things that make for peace"? Do we feel the pain of God's creatures when they are abused, tormented, or tortured by verbal barrages, by tones of resentment and scorn?

Yes, I believe there are many varieties of sons and daughters of God. There are many different kinds, both on earth and in extraterrestrial life. My hope, if I should ever encounter those who are obviously quite different from or even superior to me, is that they be more mature than I (and we earthlings) in their moral and spiritual life. And I hope this for my own selfish protection! In this hope for their greater maturity I see my need to grow and mature.

SUGGESTIONS FOR GROUP DISCUSSION

1. What implications can you draw from the discovery that all the building blocks for life [ammonia, methane, oxygen, hydrogen, nitrogen, amino acids, etc.] found on earth are also found throughout the universe?

2. Which characteristics in the following list qualify as being in the image of God: aesthetics, size, intelligence, physical

form (shape), molecular structure, color, morality, ability to experience fellowship with God? Why did you choose your list?

3. List six different professions whose members are interested in extraterrestrial intelligence. What could possibly be learned from such space beings? Could Christians learn about God from intelligent beings who may differ molecularly from us?

4. Suppose there are intelligent beings on other planets of God's universe: What moral rating do you think they might give us earthlings in our use of natural resources, family life, theological openness, international relationships?

5. How can we interpret Jesus Christ as the Lord of the universe? Would God's revelation on earth be consistent with or differ from a revelation on another planet? Why? Is Christ the logos, the same being yesterday, today, and forever throughout the universe?

6. Think of half a dozen different (unique) ways in which orders of worship could be developed to increase our awareness of the greatness and love of God.

7. Why do some earthlings respond in fear or apprehension to the idea of extraterrestrial intelligent beings? How can your faith help overcome such fears and suspicions?

NOTES

[1]*Time Magazine,* September 2, 1974, p. 88.

[2]Carl Sagan (author of *Cosmic Connection* [Garden City, N.Y.: Doubleday 1973]; see p. 188) is an astronomer and exobiologist at Cornell. He has worked on the space vehicles (Viking crafts) which will land on Mars on July 4, 1976; He designed the plaque attached to Pioneer 10 and 11.

[3]*Ibid.,* p. 196; also *Other Worlds,* (New York: Bantam Books, 1975); cf. John G. Taylor, *Black Holes: The End of the Universe?* (New York: Random House, 1974); Robert McCall and Issac Asimov, *Worlds in Space* (Greenwich, Conn: New York Graphics Society, 1974).

[4]Erich Von Däniken, *Chariots of the Gods?* (New York: G. P. Putnam's

Sons, 1974), p. 30.

[5] For an excellent account of this cryptogram see Walter Sullivan's *We Are Not Alone* (New York: McGraw-Hill, 1966), p. 269.

[6] Photo and description credit: National Aeronautics and Space Administration.

[7] See *Saturday Review,* November 7, 1964, p. 67.

[8] Sagan, *The Cosmic Connection,* p. 247.